THE POWER

OF

THE PAUSE

FINDING COURAGE IN CHANGE

THE POWER

OF

THE PAUSE

FINDING COURAGE IN CHANGE

BY

EFFIE SANTOS

ISBN: 978-1-961650-16-9 (Paperback)
ISBN: 978-1-961650-17-6 (Hardcover)
ISBN: 978-1-961650-15-2 (e-book)

Printed in the United States of America.
Published in the United States by GeeMorgan Publishing

First printing edition 2024.
All inquiries about this book can be sent to the author at
Inspire@effiesantos.com or EffieSantos@geemorganpublishing.com

For more information, or to book an event, visit the website: www.effiesantos.com
GeeMorgan Publishing
19046 Bruce B Downs Blvd #1016,
Tampa, FL 33647
www.geemorganpublishing.com

CONTENTS

INTRODUCTION
Embrace the Pause 9

PART 1
UNDERSTANDING THE PAUSE
THE CONCEPT AND ITS IMPORTANCE 13
CHAPTER 1
WHY PAUSE? 14
CHAPTER 2
EFFIE'S EVOLUTION 19
CHAPTER 3
EMBRACING THE STRENGTH OF SLOWING DOWN 25
CHAPTER 4
REFLECTIVE PAUSES 35

PART 2
INTENTIONAL PAUSES
FROM CORPORATE TO ENTREPRENEUR 43
CHAPTER 5
THE JOURNEY FROM FINANCE NOVICE TO EMPOWERING MENTOR . 44
CHAPTER 6
GROWTH BEYOND THE GRIND.. 52

PART 3
UNEXPECTED AND UNWANTED PAUSES
NAVIGATING LOSS 63
CHAPTER 7
CONFRONTING LIFE'S UNEXPECTED TWISTS 64
CHAPTER 8
THE HEALING PATH.. 77

CHAPTER 9

    STANDING TOGETHER 85

PART 4

THE GIFTS OF THE PAUSE

HARNESSING THE POWER 89

    CHAPTER 10

        STABLE GROUNDS 90

    CHAPTER 11

        CREATING COLLECTIVE RESILIENCE............................... 96

    CHAPTER 12

        GRATEFUL REFLECTIONS... 104

PART 5

NURTURING THE PAUSE

MOVING AHEAD 109

    CHAPTER 13

        FROM LEMONS TO LESSONS 110

    CHAPTER 14

        MADISON'S LEGACY 118

    EPILOGUE

        JOURNEYING TOGETHER 125

    ACKNOWLEDGEMENTS 131

    REFERENCES... 133

DEDICATION

To My Strongest Supporters, this book is for you!

To my badass mom, you are the true pillar of our family and my hero. Your love has been my safety net, catching me every time life tried to knock me down. You have been there for every laugh, every tear, and everything in between. You have taught me what it means to be strong and resilient, just by being you. Thank you for every hug, every lesson, and all the love you have poured into me.

To Lester, my partner, my rock, and my greatest cheerleader in this wild adventure we call life. Your love has been my shelter, and your faith in me has lifted me up, helping me see the greatness within when I doubted myself. I am deeply thankful for your ongoing belief in me and for accepting me in all my forms. Side by side, facing whatever comes, we are unstoppable —our love proves it every day.

To Athena, my brilliant daughter, your big heart, resilience, and pursuit of excellence makes my heart swell with pride. You have navigated life's challenges with grace, showing wisdom beyond your years, and you continue to be an incredible role model for Madison. The way you are always there for me, with understanding and love, has fused our hearts in a bond that cannot be broken, making us not just mother and daughter but the truest of friends.

To my sweet and sassy Madi, my "sweet cheeks," not a day goes by that I do not feel the void of your absence. Your vibrant spirit, full of joy and kindness, still shines brightly around us. Your big heart, always there to lend a helping hand, left an everlasting impression on our lives and countless others. Your laughter, your warmth, and those unforgettable blue eyes keep our world aglow. Athena, Yaya, Lester, and I carry your dreams forward, living out your hopes as you guide us from above, holding you close in our hearts where you will stay forever.

To all of you, my heart is full because of your love and support. I cherish each moment and memory. I love you most!

INTRODUCTION

Embrace the Pause

Life, with all its unexpected twists and heartfelt revelations, has shown me the profound value of taking a moment to pause. This book, *"The Power of the Pause,"* is not just a narrative; it is an invitation to explore the depths and nuances of pausing. Through these pages, we will delve into how moments of stillness can dramatically transform our lives, offering new perspectives, insights, and even the unexpected joy found in the most idiosyncratic of pauses.

Pausing is truly an art. It represents a momentary halt in our relentless pursuits, providing a precious opportunity to step back, catch our breath, and view our lives from a broader perspective. It is in these pauses that we discover clarity amidst confusion and find wisdom in silence. Often, it begins with a simple yet profound question: "What am I doing and why?"

Have you ever found yourself pondering the 'what ifs' of your life, fantasizing about a different career path, or envisioning a new lifestyle? What if there was a strategy, a secret to turning those thoughts into reality? If so, this book is your guide.

"The Power of the Pause" elevates the concept of a pause from a mere break to an intentional period of reflection and reassessment. It

is about consciously deciding to take a step back to reflect on our current position and the direction we wish to head towards. It is a time for learning, evolving, and, from my own experiences, transforming. My life has been punctuated by several such pauses, each leading me down new paths filled with invaluable lessons. I invite you to join me on this journey, to understand the profound impact and potential of these pauses. One of my most recent pauses was propelled by an unimaginable loss that halted my world, teaching me the essence of true pause—a period to grieve, reflect, and eventually find new ways to engage with the world. This profound experience highlighted the guiding light of a loved one's spirit, accompanying me on my path to healing and rediscovery.

Pausing is about carving out space in our hectic schedules for deep reflection and self-assessment. Yet, it is far from being passive. Effective pausing involves planning and questioning—identifying what brings joy, understanding our strengths, and aligning with our passions and purposes. A pivotal moment in my life was the transition from a stable, 25-year career in finance, to the vibrant world of entrepreneurship. This wasn't merely a career change but a bold dive into innovation, self-discovery, and applying my skills in new, exciting ways.

With our "*Power of the Pause Journal*" in hand, let's embark on this journey together. This journal is more than a mere notebook; it is a companion on our adventure, ready to hold our deepest thoughts, reflections, and even those light-hearted musings that come along the way. As we venture through this book, I invite you to reflect on the moments when a pause in your life brought significant insight or change, consider the impact of constant busyness, and remember those times when a seemingly small pause redirected your path.

This book intertwines my personal stories with the universal experience of pausing, illustrating how these moments are not just breaks but pivotal turning points. From career shifts to navigating grief, each pause has been a step toward growth and resilience. In the upcoming chapters, we will explore the multifaceted nature of pauses, showing you how to use them to gain clarity and direction. This guide is crafted for those contemplating major life changes, embarking on new ventures, or seeking deeper self-awareness. The pause is a powerful tool at your disposal.

Remember, the significance of a pause stretches beyond life-altering events to the everyday decisions where we choose to step back and reflect. We will delve into strategies for embracing pauses, covering reflection, retreats, and rediscovering joy. You will discover how journaling can facilitate decision-making and how to find your passions in unexpected places.

The butterfly, our symbol of transformation, reminds us of the beauty and strength that arise from well-timed pauses. As you begin this journey, gather your courage, take a deep breath, and open your journal. Each chapter will unveil layers of self-awareness, provide practical tools for facing challenges, and inspire you to build the life you desire. Trust in the process, embrace the journey and let *"The Power of the Pause"* guide you to clarity, joy, and abundance. As you turn these pages, may you find resonance, inspiration, and 'aha' moments that compel you to keep reading. Welcome to *"The Power of the Pause,"* a journey where we will discover that within every pause lies the potential for remarkable transformation and growth.

Disclaimer: Throughout this book, you will notice I refer to my daughter as Madi or Madison interchangeably. Please understand it is the same beloved person—these are just the affectionate names we have always used. I want to clarify that I am not a healthcare or mental health professional. The experiences and insights I share are drawn from my own life, reflecting what I have found beneficial during my journey of grief and healing. Every individual mentioned in this book and its accompanying journal has given their consent to be named or has chosen to appear anonymously. In certain cases, names have been changed to respect the wishes of those preferring to remain anonymous. At the end of nearly every chapter, you will find five reflective questions. These are intended to encourage you to delve deeper into your own experiences and insights, ideally, with the *"Power of the Pause Journal"* by your side. This journal, designed to complement the book, is available wherever books are sold, including where you found this book.

Welcome to our shared journey.

With All My Love,

ES

PART 1

UNDERSTANDING THE PAUSE

THE CONCEPT AND ITS IMPORTANCE

CHAPTER 1

WHY PAUSE?

In our journey through life, we encounter various moments of pause. These pauses, whether intentional, unexpected, or chosen for personal growth, serve as pivotal points that can lead to profound insights and transformative experiences. This chapter explores the types of pauses and their significance in our lives, providing a foundation for the strategies and reflections that follow.

Intentional Pauses

Intentional pauses are the breaths between life's notes, the quiet spaces where we choose to step off the carousel of our daily grind and into a moment of stillness. These pauses are acts of courage, a declaration that for this moment, our well-being takes precedence. They are the deliberate choices we make to disconnect, reflect, and engage deeply with our inner selves.

Imagine standing at the edge of a serene lake at dawn, the world around you just beginning to stir. This tranquility, this deliberate stillness, is akin to the intentional pause. It is in these moments that we permit ourselves to simply be—to listen to our thoughts, to reckon with our feelings, and to realign with our core values and goals.

Intentional pauses are not about doing nothing; they are about doing what matters. It is the conscious decision to meditate in the morning, to turn off our devices and turn towards our loved ones, or to take a solitary walk, letting the beauty of nature inspire us. These pauses give us the space to breathe, contemplate our life's direction, and make decisions that truly resonate with who we are and who we aspire to be.

In these chosen moments of pause, we find clarity. Like the artist stepping back to view their painting, we gain perspective on our lives. We see the brushstrokes of our daily decisions, the colors of our emotions, and the canvas of our relationships. From this vantage point, we can determine which elements of our life enhance our masterpiece and which detract from it.

An intentional pause is an opportunity to reconnect with the essence of our being. It is a time to ask ourselves the hard questions: Are we living in harmony with our values? Are our actions aligned with our goals? What changes do we need to make to live more authentically?

By embracing intentional pauses, we invite joy, creativity, and purpose into our lives. We learn to navigate the complexities of our existence with grace and resilience. These pauses become the steppingstones to a more mindful, fulfilled, and balanced life.

So, let us cherish these intentional pauses. Let us make room for them amidst the hustle and bustle of our daily routines. It is in these moments of deliberate stillness that we discover ourselves anew, find the strength to pursue our dreams, and cultivate a life that truly reflects the depth of our spirit.

Unexpected Pauses

Life's journey is punctuated by unexpected pauses—sudden, unforeseen events that bring our forward motion to a standstill. These moments, though initially challenging, hold within them the seeds of growth and discovery. They demand that we confront our present reality, push us to adapt, and, in doing so, reveal strengths within us that we might never have recognized otherwise.

In facing these unplanned interruptions, we are invited to take stock of our lives, to question, and to recalibrate. These pauses act as a mirror, reflecting to us the truths about our lives that the constant motion obscures. Within the quiet of these unexpected breaks, there is a profound opportunity to learn about ourselves, to grow in resilience, and to emerge with a clearer vision of where we want to go.

Unplanned pauses are life's way of nudging us towards introspection and realignment. They remind us that growth is not just found in relentless progress but is also found in the reflective quiet of a pause. Here, stripped of the distractions of our daily routines, we can find the clarity and resolve to move forward in ways more aligned with our deepest values and aspirations.

Let us view these moments not as detours but as integral parts of our journey, rich with potential for insight and transformation. In embracing the unexpected pauses life presents, we open ourselves to a deeper understanding of our path and purpose, ready to navigate the complexities of life with a renewed sense of direction and strength.

Pauses for Personal Growth

Certain pauses in our lives are deliberately chosen for the sake of personal growth. These are the moments we consciously carve out from our daily hustle to dedicate to learning new skills, enhancing our health, or diving into new hobbies. Such pauses are, in essence, investments in our well-being, pivotal for nurturing a state of wellness and for fostering a life that is not only richer but also more rewarding.

By setting aside time for these developmental pauses, we prioritize our self-care and personal enrichment. It is in these stretches of deliberate stillness that we find the freedom to explore, to experiment, and to expand our horizons. Whether it it's mastering a new language, cultivating a meditation practice, or embarking on artistic endeavors, each chosen pause is a steppingstone toward a more vibrant and fulfilling existence.

These periods of intentional growth remind us that to live fully, we must sometimes slow down. They teach us the value of patience, the importance of curiosity, and the beauty of self-discovery. In dedicating time to nurture our interests and health, we not only enhance our own lives but also enrich the lives of those around us with our renewed energy and perspective.

Embracing these chosen pauses for personal development allows us to reconnect with our passions and rediscover the joy of learning. It is a journey that encourages us to embrace change, celebrate progress, and cherish the path of continuous self-improvement.

Prepare to embark on a journey of discovery with your "*Power of the Pause Journal*". Find a cozy spot where you can freely express your thoughts and curiosities. Imagine each page as a blank canvas awaiting the dance of your pen, ready to capture the essence of your reflective moments. This is your opportunity to shine, delve into the depths of your journey, and uncover the treasures hidden within.

As you begin, ponder on these questions to reflect on your life experiences:

1. Recall a time when taking a break or altering your routine led to new insights. What revelations came to you?
2. Identify the activities that invigorate you, making you feel truly alive and absorbed.
3. Consider whether there has been a moment you felt compelled to try something novel or different. What was the source of this inspiration?
4. Think back to an instance where stepping away from your hectic schedule provided a new outlook. Can you describe what this fresh perspective was?
5. Reflect on how you typically respond to unforeseen changes or obstacles in your daily life.

This exploration of pauses and their significance is not just an exercise; it is an enlightening and empowering journey that could potentially transform your perspective on life and its myriad pauses.

CHAPTER 2

EFFIE'S EVOLUTION

From Cosmetology Dreams to Financial Innovation

My venture into the world of finance began where you might least expect—in a high school cosmetology class. Among hair dryers and lively conversations, I nurtured a dream to one day open a grand salon. This ambition was not new; it echoed childhood days spent organizing "meetings" in a treehouse, a clear sign of my innate drive to lead and innovate.

This path veered unexpectedly when a client mentioned her son's job at a bank, highlighting how it supported his education. This insight sparked a pivotal change. Soon after, I secured a part-time teller position at Barnett Bank, a role that promised more than just a job—it was a steppingstone toward my larger aspirations.

Balancing this new role with my cosmetology license and college studies, I was on a path filled with promise. Yet, life had other plans. At 19, my family faced a profound challenge: my dad's diagnosis with stage 4 lung cancer. His illness brought a pause to my education, as I focused on supporting my family during this trying time. My dad's pride in my banking job, expressed before his passing, became a source of strength and motivation in the difficult days that followed.

Despite never returning to college—a decision that still tugs at me—I climbed the finance ladder, driven by determination and leadership skills perhaps first honed in that childhood treehouse. My 25-year career in finance was defined by leadership, team building, and notably, mentoring. Beyond guiding colleagues through financial complexities, I took pride in helping them achieve their life goals, a fulfillment that extended beyond office walls through volunteer work, sharing my journey to light the way for others.

Empowering women to pursue their entrepreneurial dreams particularly resonated with me, echoing my aspirations. It was incredibly fulfilling to guide others to find their paths, just as I sought mine.

However, a familiar restlessness for new beginnings began to grow. Despite achieving financial stability and respect, the urge to create something from scratch—to lead without limits—became undeniable. My entrepreneurial spirit once dreamt of while being in a large salon, now sought a broader horizon.

Choosing to leave the finance world to start my own business was a decision steeped in years of reflection, experience, and a deep desire to embrace my roots of innovation and leadership. This leap into entrepreneurship marked a return to my passion for creation and a challenge to the traditional security found in corporate life.

This journey of twists, turns, and newfound paths has been a testament to the power of resilience, the importance of embracing change, and the courage to venture into the unknown. It is a story I share to inspire others to consider what might be possible if we dare to let go of the familiar and embrace the new with open arms.

Braving the Pause: Accepting Courage in Stillness

Embracing a pause requires courage. It asks us to be still in a world that values constant motion. This section delves into the bravery needed to accept pauses, showing how stillness can be a powerful ally in understanding ourselves and our place in the world.

In the constant march of life, where each second propels us to keep moving, embracing a pause embodies a profound act of courage. It signifies a conscious decision to halt, to step away from the unending push of daily obligations, and to find strength in stillness. Pausing is not merely a break but a skillful defiance against a world that seldom stops to breathe. It creates a sanctuary amidst turmoil, a space for reflection and realignment, where we can rediscover our most authentic selves.

Consider the significance of a true pause, one that allows for deep introspection rather than a brief cessation. Our modern lives rarely acknowledge the transformative power of quietude. These moments are not just empty spaces in our schedules but are rich with potential for personal growth and enlightenment.

Embracing the pause has been a pivotal part of my journey. It involves mustering courage in moments of quiet, attuning to the subtle inner voices that get drowned out by life's noise. It offers a precious opportunity to reassess our paths, reconnect with our innermost desires, and, if necessary, forge a new direction.

In the stillness of a pause, we encounter our unvarnished selves, stripped of societal roles and external expectations. This is where we confront the fundamental questions of our identity and aspirations. It is a fertile ground where dreams are nurtured, and meaningful transformation can take root.

However, the journey into stillness is not without its challenges. It is in these silent stretches that our doubts and fears often surface, bringing to light the insecurities we might prefer to keep hidden. Like illuminating a darkened room, a pause allows everything to come into view, demanding that we face our truths, no matter how uncomfortable. Yet, it is precisely in this illumination that we find clarity and the opportunity for genuine insight and change.

The Transformative Power of Letting Go

In my journey, deciding to step away from the familiar path of a long-term career embodied a significant pause, filled with both apprehension and a deep sense of yearning for more. This pause, fraught with uncertainty, prompted a period of deep reflection on my core values and a keen listening to that inner voice seeking a new direction. Despite the fear, this pause became a pivotal moment, propelling me into a new chapter and an exploration of the unknown. Pauses serve as bridges to our intuition, that guiding voice within us that too often gets lost in the hustle and bustle of everyday life. It is in the quiet of a pause that this voice becomes clear, providing wisdom and pointing us toward our true north.

Looking at nature, we see how pauses are integral to cycles of renewal and growth. Winter represents a pause for the earth, a necessary period of rest that precedes the vibrant awakening of spring. This analogy reminds us that a pause is not a void but a period brimming with potential and preparation, essential for what comes next.

The act of embracing a pause also teaches us the art of release. It involves letting go of our compulsion to control every detail of our existence, trusting in the journey, and remaining open to the myriad paths our lives might take. Learning to relinquish control is indeed challenging; it forces us to confront uncertainty and find peace in not knowing what the future holds.

Reflect on moments in your life when a pause has ushered in something meaningful. Perhaps it was a moment of quiet that healed a rift, or a hiatus that offered a fresh outlook. Whether monumental or minor, these pauses have the power to shape our lives in profound and lasting ways.

Reflective Journeys: Navigating Life's Pauses

Let us explore these reflective points in your *"Power of the Pause Journal"*. This journey is not just about self-reflection; it is an invitation to uncover the profound insights and decisions that shape our lives.

Here are some reflective points to guide you:

1. Recall a moment when a pause led to a pivotal insight or decision. What was the revelation?

2. Consider the impact of constant busyness. How might your life transform if you embraced more pauses?

3. Identify an area where you aspire to be bolder. What hurdles are in your way?

4. Reflect on a significant risk you have taken. How did taking a moment to pause influence your decision?

5. Picture your most courageous self. How can integrating more pauses into your life help you evolve into this person?

As we delve into the essence of the pause, we recognize that these moments are not mere interruptions but the foundation of growth and self-discovery. They are the silent beats that give rhythm to our life's melody, the spaces where our truest selves take shape.

This chapter is your invitation to embrace life's pauses. See them as opportunities to reconnect with your inner self, to find clarity between the chaos, and to chart a course towards a life that truly resonates with your soul. The journey of a thousand miles begins with a single step, and often, that step is a pause.

Welcome to the pathway of the pause— a journey where stillness speaks volumes, where quiet moments hold the key to our deepest transformations, and where every pause is a chance to rewrite our story. Let us embrace this journey together, discovering the courage that lies in stillness and the strength that comes from simply being.

CHAPTER 3

EMBRACING THE STRENGTH OF SLOWING DOWN

Our lives often resemble a relentless race, with moments of pause feeling more like a luxury than a necessity. Yet, there is undeniable strength in slowing down, a magic that unfolds when we press pause on life's fast-forward button. Slowing down in a fast-paced world is a strength, not a weakness. It does not mean you are doing less.

It is about enjoying more, really soaking in your experiences, and being fully there in a way that is often missed when we are caught up in our routines. It is a path to reconnecting with oneself, to discovering clarity amidst chaos, and to living a life that truly resonates with one's soul. It is a journey into the calm within, an exploration of self that transcends mere idleness to become a profound act of discovery.

We are going to look at how taking it easy can bring out the best in us, like being more aware, connecting on a deeper level with people, and feeling more thankful for the here and now. You will get to rethink how you are living your life and ask yourself why we often think being busy all the time is something to aim for, even when it leaves us feeling worn out and out of touch with who we are.

You will find tips on how to take things slower in your day-to-day, how to be more mindful, and how to focus on what is really important. We will talk about how to gracefully say 'no' to taking on too much, the good in setting up calming routines, and the need for time to just think and rest.

Choosing to embrace one's inner tranquility is essentially a commitment to nurturing one's well-being, relationships, and personal development. It acknowledges that true productivity isn't measured by the swiftness of our actions but by the depth of our engagement with life. This concept goes beyond merely slowing down; it's about enriching the connection with both the world around us and the untapped potential within.

As we go through life's chapters, let us value the power of taking it slow and the peace that comes with it. Let us see success not in how fast we achieve things, but in the quality and thoughtfulness of our journey.

Embracing the Pause in a Rushed World

Is it really that simple? you might wonder. Indeed, finding that serene space and your sanctuary amidst the whirlwind of life is about allowing yourself to pause, to immerse in the moment, and to simply exist. This calm within serves as a quiet rebellion against the incessant rush, offering a secluded space to disconnect and breathe deeply.

Facing the silence can indeed be daunting. Our minds often equate stillness with unproductivity, urging us to keep moving, to do more. But let me share a personal revelation: it is within these moments of stillness that we uncover our hidden strengths.

Reflecting on a pivotal moment in my career, I recall seeking clarity amidst confusion. It was in the tranquility of a park, allowing the world to continue its orbit without me, that insights began to crystallize. This sense of peace extended to my walks with Lucy, my furry companion. Unlike the usual rush, where a Bluetooth device in my ear dictated the pace, our strolls became an exercise in mindfulness. With Lucy the cockapoo by my side, we embraced the slow rhythm of life, taking in nature's tranquility. Our walks were not just about physical exercise but about connecting with the environment and engaging in the lost art of simply being present. These moments of pause became my sanctuary, a place where thoughts could flow, and insights could form unbidden amidst the beauty of the natural world.

This practice is far from the distracted, hurried laps we often associate with dog walking. It is an exercise in mindfulness, appreciating the gentle warmth of the sun, the playful breeze stirring my hair, and the sweet serenade of the birds. Each butterfly that flutters by feels like a gentle 'hello' from Madi, accompanying us in spirit.

It is during these leisurely walks that my life takes a turn from the ordinary. I find myself in deep, heartfelt conversations with Madi, my beloved youngest daughter whose life was tragically cut short at 19 due to a car accident. To some, speaking to a loved one who has passed might seem unconventional, but for me, it is a cherished method of keeping our connection alive, a testament to the enduring bond we share. It is in these moments of dialogue with Madi that the extraordinary occurs—butterflies circling me as if delivering messages, stumbling upon "Happy Birthday Madison" signs, or overhearing a mother's farewell to her daughter, "Have a good day Madi," echoing my sentiments. These instances are not coincidences but profound communications, revealing the depth of connection that can emerge when we truly slow down and attune to the present.

These pauses bring a symphony of heart and mind, sparking waves of creativity and insight. Whether it is generating ideas for Madi's Movement, the nonprofit founded in her honor, or navigating my path to wellness, clarity becomes my steadfast ally. Remarkably, some of the most innovative concepts for this book were conceived during these moments of reflection.

The essence of tranquility has become my most profound instructor, teaching me the value of stillness in fostering progress and peace. It has illuminated the truth that sometimes the most significant step forward is taken by standing still, listening to the hush, and reveling in life's simplest joys.

On another walk, an epiphany struck me like a bolt of clarity— mindfulness needed to become a more integral part of my life's fabric. This realization was nothing short of transformative. You might wonder how this book came into existence. It all started with a gentle push from my husband, Lester, who believed it was time to share our odyssey of challenges and victories with the world.

As I pondered over his suggestion during our serene morning walks, I recognized the immense potential our stories held to inspire and impact others. It was a moment of truth, a call to action that could not be ignored.

These tranquil moments are not merely for introspection, they are the birthplaces of creativity and vision. They have unveiled the sheer potency of taking pauses—to listen, to absorb, and to evolve. Unbeknownst to me, I was on the cusp of a significant transformation. My days, much like yours, were a frenzy of activities, commitments, and responsibilities, leaving me to yearn for a breather, for 'me time.'

This realization led to a pivotal shift. Breaking free from the cycle of perpetual motion and the ingrained belief that busyness equated to living was daunting yet necessary. It was an internal urging for a deeper, more meaningful existence that propelled me to alter my trajectory. Yes, there were hiccups along the way, moments when the old pace attempted to regain dominance. However, each return to the essence of tranquility helped me regain my balance.

This journey, marked by moments of pause and introspection, has not only shaped the narrative of this book but also transformed my approach to life. It is a testament to the power of slowing down, creating space for what truly matters, and the remarkable clarity that comes with embracing the calm within.

Beneath the surface of a successful finance career, my spirit was restless, whispering of undiscovered paths and new beginnings. This sense of anticipation, of a change on the horizon, grew within me, challenging the comfort of my well-worn professional cocoon. For twenty-five years, banking had been my world, yet a persistent voice within me insisted, "Effie, there is more out there for you... it is time to truly soar." Heeding that call took years, but eventually, the message became too loud to ignore.

A pivotal moment arrived, crystallizing my need for change. My career in finance, once a perfect fit, no longer aligned with the person I was becoming. I realized that beyond the familiar lay a world brimming with potential, waiting for me to explore. It was with this realization that I embraced my first intentional pause, unknowingly opening the door to a realm of possibilities.

Embarking on this journey starts with a critical examination of our lives. I challenge you to look at your schedule and ask yourself the following:

- ❖ What matters most to me?
- ❖ Do my daily activities reflect my deepest goals and desires?

When I boldly followed this advice and answered these questions for myself, I drastically reduced my commitments by 70%, a decision as liberating as surfacing for air after a deep dive. This dramatic shift allowed the light of new possibilities to penetrate the organized chaos of my life, and further illuminated a path forward I had never imagined possible.

In the newfound chapters of my life, a simple, yet profound change marked the beginning of a revolutionary journey. I made the conscious decision to start my mornings in tranquility, sitting on my porch with a steaming cup of coffee in hand, devoid of any digital distractions. Just me, my thoughts, and the quiet morning air. Initially, I questioned the productivity of such pauses—could this really be a worthwhile use of my time? The answer, it turned out, was a resounding yes. This practice of morning stillness did not just alter my daily routine; it transformed my entire outlook on life.

Embracing these moments of pause became my gateway to clarity and mindfulness. Far from being a waste of time, it was a period of recharge and reconnection with the essentials of life. My porch became more than just a physical space; it evolved into a sanctuary for reflection, a space where dreams could breathe and take shape.

This narrative serves as a testament to the power inherent in slowing down—an act of self-care and personal evolution that is both brave and necessary. It is in the quietude that we find the space to unfurl our true selves, to discover the extraordinary in the ordinary.

As you embark on your journey of embracing the slower moments, I encourage you to assess your daily commitments. Are they in harmony with your deepest dreams and goals? Is there space in your life for stillness, for that vital pause? The magic of intentional pauses lies in their ability to unlock doors to clarity and invigoration that we never knew existed.

Within the embrace of the calm, we often stumble upon an unexpected reservoir of strength. It may seem counterintuitive at first— our society equates strength with constant motion and productivity. Yet, there lies a profound form of strength in stillness, a resilience that springs from the depths of our being, waiting to be acknowledged and embraced. This inner fortitude, discovered in moments of pause, is a reminder that our true power often lies not in relentless activity but in the ability to be still with ourselves.

Unveiling Your Inner Strength and Insight through Stillness

In the embrace of tranquility, as we allow ourselves the grace of presence, a unique form of resilience begins to flourish within us. These quiet moments become lessons in listening deeply to the subtle guidance of our intuition, which nudges us gently towards our truest paths. It is in the embrace of silence that we connect with a deep well of wisdom, an internal compass that steers us towards decisions made with clarity and conviction.

The sanctuary of stillness is where we fortify our mental and emotional resilience. This quietude is not passive; it is an active engagement with our innermost fears, doubts, and uncertainties. Facing these with compassion and an open heart transforms our approach to life's challenges, endowing us with the adaptability and resilience required to navigate through them.

Much like physical strength is honed through consistent exercise, our inner resilience is cultivated through each deliberate pause we take. These pauses teach us the value of self-trust and patience, illuminating the truth that personal growth and transformation often germinate in the silent, reflective stretches of our lives. They embolden us to venture into the unknown, to embrace risks, and to pursue our dreams with unwavering determination.

This journey of building inner strength is ongoing, a path we walk throughout our lives. Every pause we take is an opportunity to deepen our resilience, to reinforce our belief in ourselves, and to foster a trust that is rooted deeply within. With each pause, we grow more in tune with our inner potential, inching closer to manifesting the life we dream of.

These moments of pause have become my sanctuary, a space where evolution and rejuvenation intertwine. They remind us of the beauty that lies in stillness, offering us the freedom to explore and express our authentic selves.

Thus, I invite you to welcome the calm, to discover within its quietude the transformative power to strengthen, to connect deeply with your true essence, and to consciously shape your path forward. It is about finding and recognizing the extraordinary in the ordinary, allowing yourself the space to explore the vastness of your true potential.

As you delve deeper, I encourage you to embrace a moment of introspection with your journal by your side. Find that special nook that feels like a refuge, and allow the following questions to illuminate your path:

1. Reflect on the essence of inner strength during moments of stillness. How do you define it within the quiet?

2. Bring to mind a moment when peace and quiet unexpectedly filled you with a sense of power. What was that experience like?

3. Identify the barriers that prevent you from integrating more pauses into your daily life. What are they, and why do they exist?

4. Recall a pause that culminated in a significant realization. What were you engaged in at that moment?

5. Honor the insights gained during times of tranquility. What have these moments revealed to you about your inner self?

Let the stillness be your guide. Allow the serene moments to weave their magic throughout your existence, inviting clarity, creativity, and direction to flow freely. These pauses are not mere gaps; they are fertile ground for purpose, joy, and boundless opportunities. Embrace the walks, cherish the conversations, and let the tranquility within reveal its transformative power. This journey, adorned with pauses and reflections, is one of immense value, and I walk alongside you, every step of the way.

CHAPTER 4

REFLECTIVE PAUSES

Reflection is a crucial aspect of pauses. Through reflective practices, we can examine our past actions, learn from our experiences, and shape a future that aligns with our deepest aspirations. This section offers strategies for using reflective pauses as a tool for personal and professional growth.

Reflecting to Shape Your Future

Reflective pauses are powerful moments where we take stock of our lives, contemplating our current paths and the alignment of our actions with our deepest desires. I encourage you to take a moment, breathe deeply, and assess where you stand in life. Are you moving in a direction that feels right? Identify areas that seem out of sync or that crave your attention. Let your thoughts and feelings flow onto paper without censorship, capturing the essence of your experiences, both the triumphs and the challenges, in their rawest form.

For me, the journey began with committing time to sit quietly, carving out a sanctuary for introspection. This process unfolded gradually, as I dedicated myself to daily reflection, noting my thoughts and emotions without judgment. This practice helped me understand my desires for change more clearly. It is essential to remember that this process is not about achieving perfection; it is about forging a deeper connection with your aspirations and recognizing your needs.

Now, turn your attention to your dreams and what you yearn to achieve. What are the changes you long to make? What dreams have been gently prodding you? Give yourself the freedom to explore these questions openly. Write about your dreams, allowing your pen to move uninhibited, and your thoughts to soar.

Once you have identified your dreams, ponder their significance. Why are they important to you? What values do they reflect, and how do they enhance your sense of fulfillment? To gain deeper insight into these connections, engage in this activity:

1. Place each dream on a separate sheet and lay them out before you.
2. For every dream, note the underlying values. For example, if you dream of starting a bakery, values might include creativity, autonomy, and community connection.
3. Use colored pens or markers to draw connections between each dream and its associated values, adding symbols or sketches that resonate with you.
4. This visual representation will help you see how your aspirations and values interlink, guiding you to understand their role in your happiness.

This is not just about listing goals; it is a dive into what motivates and drives you, sparking a deeper enthusiasm for your aspirations. Approach this exploration with honesty and bravery. The more you understand yourself, the more prepared you are to face and overcome any obstacles.

Consider the feasibility of the changes you wish to see. While dreaming big is encouraged, it is equally important to root these dreams in reality. For instance, if you aim to run a marathon but are new to running, start with shorter distances, gradually increasing your endurance. Or, if starting a business is your goal but financial stability is a concern, think about launching it as a side project or researching funding opportunities.

Planning for possible challenges allows you to develop strategies for overcoming them, transforming your aspirations from dreams into tangible objectives. This preparation provides you with the mindset and tools needed to actualize your dreams.

In the midst of contemplating a significant career shift from the security of finance to the uncertainties of entrepreneurship, I found myself engulfed in a storm of emotions. My journal, which I affectionately dubbed my Best Fearless Friend (BFF), transformed into a haven for my swirling thoughts, fears, and aspirations. Initially skeptical about the value of journaling—viewing it as perhaps a frivolous use of time—I was soon proven wrong. Embracing journaling opened up a private space where I could freely express myself, laying out my thoughts and feelings without concern for the formalities of writing. This practice became pivotal, a part of my daily routine that offered clarity and insight into my deepest desires.

Journaling served as a mirror, reflecting my passions and the activities that filled me with joy, while also helping me identify and release the tasks that no longer served me. This process was not just about self-discovery; it was an act of liberation, stripping away the layers of doubt and societal expectations to uncover the true essence of my aspirations.

The journey of self-reflection requires brutal honesty, a willingness to confront your unvarnished truths. It is a personal voyage that challenges you to meet yourself as you are, warts and all. I encourage you to embark on this path of self-exploration. The clarity and self-understanding that emerge from such honesty can be profoundly transformative.

Through my reflective journey, the significance of self-compassion and patience became crystal clear. Navigating this path is a delicate dance between embracing vulnerability and discovering strength, inching closer to the courage I yearned for. Yes, there were moments of doubt and nights filled with introspection, questioning the correctness of my chosen direction. Yet, through these times, a simple mantra became my beacon: "I am worthy and deserving of a life filled with purpose and joy." This affirmation, repeated with conviction, reminded me to extend the same kindness and empathy to myself that I would offer a friend in similar straits.

Embracing the Path to Self-Compassion

To cultivate self-compassion on my path of change, I embraced practices such as journaling, mindfulness, relaxation, and celebrating every small victory. These habits fostered resilience and curiosity, guiding me gently through the transformative process.

I encourage you, as you undertake your own period of reflection, to nurture kindness towards yourself. Acknowledge each stumble with gentleness, honor your progress, and approach this journey of transformation with an open and resilient heart.

The true essence of a reflective pause lies not in the quest for instant solutions or shortcuts through life's complexities. It revolves around taking the time to slow down, to introspect, and to deeply understand one's desires and the changes one wishes to see in their life. It's about establishing a strong foundation for meaningful change, enhancing self-awareness, and clarifying one's dreams and values.

Consider the analogy of constructing a house; you would not begin with the roof. Similarly, significant life shifts require more than just spur-of-the-moment decisions or a shallow grasp of our ambitions. A robust foundation of self-awareness ensures that our transformations are not just beneficial momentarily but result in enduring personal growth.

This reflective practice equips individuals with the tools to establish such a foundation. By allocating time to delve into their desires and understand the underlying motivations, they are essentially creating a blueprint for the life they earnestly wish to lead. Possessing this blueprint, the journey to constructing a life filled with satisfaction and happiness becomes more straightforward and attainable.

Remember, the journey of reflection is continuous, a path filled with introspection, self-exploration, and growth. The destination is crucial, but so is the journey itself. Cherish each step and let the insights you gain about yourself inform the changes you aim to implement.

As you progress through this chapter, remain receptive to the surprises along the way. Trust in your inner guidance and intuition to lead you towards changes that truly align with your essence.

During my reflective interlude, I discovered a newfound love for nature—a revelation for someone who always viewed themselves as a city girl. This appreciation for the tranquility and beauty of the natural world, once overlooked, blossomed into a source of joy and renewal for me.

Reflection and self-assessment can unlock doors to deep self-understanding and change. The aim of a reflective pause is not to enforce change but to uncover your genuine self, your core desires, and your pathway to fulfillment. Approach this journey with an open mind and curiosity, allowing the process to unveil your unique discoveries and profound transformations.

Life's vast stage often thrusts us into roles we never sought— like becoming a philosopher in the quiet moments of reflection. Who would have thought that simply sitting with our thoughts could transform us into contemplative sages, mulling over life's great questions with a cup of coffee in hand?

Introspection

Let us delve into the intriguing exercise of examining our habits and routines. It is fascinating how many of our daily actions operate on autopilot, almost as if we are unwitting stars of our own 'Routine Show.' Reflecting on these patterns can sometimes feel like uncovering the comedic script of our lives, filled with episodes like spending an eternity searching for glasses that were perched on our heads all along.

In these reflective pauses, you are presented with a golden opportunity to reevaluate your life's direction. It is a chance to step back and scrutinize the patterns that have come to define you. Do these habits serve your highest good? Or are there areas where you find yourself feeling stagnant or unfulfilled? Let these introspections steer you toward the alterations necessary to align more closely with your ideal state of existence.

Before progressing to the next chapter, I encourage you to reflect on the following questions in your journal:

1. Identify the life patterns that enhance your joy and fulfillment.
2. Acknowledge the patterns that lead to frustration or disappointment.
3. Examine the triggers of your happiness or distress.
4. Assess how these patterns align with your deepest values and dreams.
5. Contemplate the adjustments needed to nurture positive patterns and transform the negative ones.

Deep dive into your daily routines and habits. Analyze them for their true impact on your journey towards authenticity and fulfillment. This is not about casting judgment but about achieving clarity and understanding yourself more profoundly.

Here's a simple exercise to further illuminate your path:

❖ Next to each listed habit, note its impact on your emotions and its contribution to your goals.

❖ Reflect on these observations. Do any habits surprise you? Are there any you wish to alter?

This exploration offers profound insights into the daily practices shaping your journey toward self-realization and fulfillment.

This is not about self-critique but about achieving clarity and a deeper acquaintance with oneself. It is a learning process to identify which habits uplift you and which may be impeding your progress. You possess the agency to sculpt your life; wield it judiciously as you advance on your path of self-discovery.

As we conclude this section, I want to underscore the incredible journey that is self-discovery. It is an ongoing exploration into our core, our values, what motivates us, and how our habits influence our everyday existence.

Revisit your journal entries, dreams, values, and the habits you have pinpointed. Embrace the hurdles, relish the discovery of your true self, and cherish the moments of reflection you have allotted for yourself. Acknowledge the surprises along the way and recognize that change, though it may be uncomfortable, often leads us closer to our genuine selves. Remember, you have the power to shape your destiny.

May these reflections and exercises spark your curiosity, deepen your introspection, and empower you to embrace your true self fully. As you step into the next chapter, remember that the path of self-discovery is rich with discovery and growth at every turn. Continue to explore, savor, and cherish each step of this extraordinary expedition.

PART 2

INTENTIONAL PAUSES

FROM CORPORATE TO ENTREPRENEUR

CHAPTER 5

THE JOURNEY FROM FINANCE NOVICE TO EMPOWERING MENTOR

My journey into the professional world started like many others—unexpectedly. At 19, I was just looking for a part-time job to help with my college expenses. That job, surprisingly, kicked off a 25-year adventure in finance. It is funny, I never planned for a career in finance, but sometimes life has its plans, tossing lemons your way when you least expect it.

Starting as a part-time teller, I worked my way through various roles in the finance sector. But the true joy came from the people side of things—building teams, supporting people, and watching them grow. It was about celebrating their successes and being there for them, really being their champion. As a woman in finance, I saw firsthand the challenges we often faced, more so than our male colleagues. According to Forbes 2018, "although 46 percent of financial services employees are women, at the executive level, it's only 15 percent". This sparked in me a desire to do more, particularly for women entrepreneurs. I wanted to be more than just a financial advisor; I aimed to be a mentor, someone who could guide and support them on their journey.

The heart of my career was about creating a sense of community and teamwork, making sure everyone felt they had a voice. Seeing someone I mentored succeed and overcome challenges was incredibly rewarding. It was proof of the impact that support and encouragement could have. This belief in lifting others as we climb became a guiding principle, shaping how I interacted, made decisions, and led.

This chapter is about those unexpected turns in our careers and lives, and how they can lead us to places we never imagined. It is about the power of reflection in understanding what we truly want and finding the courage to pursue it. As you read through my story, I hope it encourages you to embrace your journey, with all its twists and turns, and to find joy and fulfillment in supporting and uplifting those around you.

Working in finance taught me a lot about resilience and the need to adapt. It is a field where things are always shifting, and you have to be on your toes, ready to pick up new skills and adjust your plans. Embracing change and always looking to grow became a big part of my approach, whether I was leading a team, dealing with clients, or plotting out my future steps.

My time in finance was not just a job; it turned into a platform for uplifting others and setting the stage for my next big adventure— one I had not even seen coming. It was in this bustling world of numbers and strategic deals that I began to imagine what could be next, inspired by all the challenges I faced and the connections I made.

Nonprofits have always captured my heart, drawing me into a variety of roles and allowing me to witness firsthand their incredible impact on our communities. This deep involvement ignited a spark within me, a growing realization that I yearned to contribute even more significantly. It led to a pivotal moment when everything seemed to align perfectly, revealing a clear path forward in entrepreneurship—a long-held dream of mine. The more I engaged with nonprofits, the more I recognized the potential for an even greater impact. It was as if a lightbulb moment occurred, and I felt an undeniable pull toward something more ambitious. That realization marked the beginning of my journey toward pursuing a bigger dream: diving headfirst into entrepreneurship, driven by the desire to make a meaningful difference.

About five years before I left my corporate job, something started to shift inside me. My office felt smaller, and a passion was growing inside me that just couldn't be satisfied by my finance career alone. It was not that I was unhappy; I was just drawn to something else, something more. I had this dream of starting something on my own, building a business from the ground up. That pull toward entrepreneurship was strong and undeniable.

Leaping into Purpose: The Power of Dreams, Pauses, and New Beginnings

Can you picture holding onto a dream that is so vibrant and vast, simmering within you for an entire five years? It is kind of like standing at the edge of a cliff, your heart pounding, on the brink of jumping, yet there is that small voice cautioning you about the bills, the stability, and the "What if it fails?" Yet, thinking of my daughters, I was driven by the desire to show them the importance of pursuing their dreams, no matter the scale. That determination outweighed any fear I might have had.

You have probably felt this blend of thrill and apprehension at some point, right? After a lot of reflection, I was certain it was time to heed the call to carve out my path. Finance had been good to me, but I was ready for a new chapter.

I am a big believer in the power of having clear goals. With dreams fueling my resolve, I took a deliberate pause, overflowing with ideas. It was a calculated step back to sort everything out. You might wonder, "What did that entail?" I laid out a one-year plan to establish my business, which involved everything from creating a brand identity and defining services to launching a website and developing marketing materials. I aimed for a solid foundation that mirrored my identity and values. Venturing into new territory meant collaborating with experts to ensure I was on the right path, all while maintaining my corporate role. The strategy was to juggle both for a year. However, life has a way of laughing at our plans, leading to unexpected turns. But that is a story for another time!

What did taking a big pause in my life look like? It meant getting up early and staying up late, my house turning into a landscape of sticky notes, and a journal that became my confidante. Saying no to social outings and missing out on get-togethers was not easy, but I had my eyes on the prize—aligning my passion with a meaningful purpose. In this pause, a clear vision started to emerge. With my deep dive into the nonprofit sector over the years, participating in boards, committees, and working closely with non-profit clients, I saw firsthand the challenges and gaps that persisted. A fire was lit within me to fill these gaps, to be the link that could meaningfully connect corporations with nonprofits, ensuring not just their survival but their ability to flourish. My aim? To offer a stable support system for these organizations to continue making a difference.

I remember this defining moment clearly. I was at my go-to spot, the professional club I loved, with my journal and a good cup of coffee in hand. As ideas were taking shape, a simple yet profound realization dawned on me: **COMPANIES + CAUSES = IMPACT**. It was one of those moments where everything suddenly clicked into place, revealing a path that seemed destined. At that instant, I knew I had found the perfect blend of my experience, passion, and a real-world need.

Initially, I thought I could manage both my finance job and my budding enterprise for a year. But life has a way of showing us new directions. Six months down the line, I recognized that splitting my energy was not working—not because I could not handle it, but because I wanted to give my all to what truly ignited my spirit. The excitement and dedication I was pouring into my new venture made me question— why not go all in? Trusting my instincts, I decided to fully commit to my entrepreneurial dream, stepping away from finance to dive deep into my passion project. After all, it is all about following the energy that fuels you!

Shaping Your Path

Stepping into this new adventure, I brought along all the lessons and experiences that had shaped me up to that point. Aware of the hurdles ahead, my drive was not dampened; instead, I saw these challenges as opportunities for growth, each one a step towards reaching greater heights. Surrounded by the support of my loved ones, the wisdom of my mentors, and my resilience, I was more than ready to forge ahead, make a meaningful impact, and live life by my design.

Diving into the world of entrepreneurship, I embraced the significance of pauses in my journey. Each pause served as a beacon, guiding me through the tumultuous seas of starting anew. ***The fearless pause*** was my confrontation with the inner doubts and fears that whispered of failure and uncertainty. It was during these moments I found the courage to stare down these fears, to acknowledge their presence but not let them steer my course. This pause was a declaration of my resolve, a testament to my willingness to face the unknown with a bold heart.

Then there was ***the peaceful pause***, a sanctuary of calm amid the storm. It was my time to reset, breathe deeply, and recharge my spirit. Amidst the hustle and bustle of building something from the ground up, this pause was my haven, a reminder of the importance of balance and well-being. It was here, in the quiet, that I found clarity and rejuvenation, readying myself for the challenges ahead.

Lastly, ***the thoughtful pause*** served as my compass, ensuring that every step I took was aligned with my core values and objectives. It was a time for reflection, for looking inward and asking the hard questions about the direction of my journey. This pause was about intentionality, about making sure that the path I was forging not only led to success but resonated with the essence of who I am and what I stand for.

Together, these pauses formed the rhythm of my entrepreneurial symphony, each one a crucial note in the melody of my venture. They taught me that true progress is not always about moving forward but also about knowing when to stand still, to listen, and to learn. As I navigated through these pauses, I saw them not as interruptions but as opportunities for growth, empowerment, and deep, meaningful success.

Now, picture a butterfly emerging from its cocoon. That transformation, from being confined to flying free, is a lot like these pauses—growth and preparation within the cocoon leading to eventual flight. With reflection and time, we, too, can spread our wings, embracing change and setting our sights on new goals.

This journey from the corporate sphere to the entrepreneurial world has been an exploration of intentional pauses. But this narrative is not mine alone; it is a universal call to action. When paths become unclear, it is these reflective moments that can sharpen our focus and direction.

Reflective pauses were my golden hours of clarity, bridging my structured corporate life with the vibrant uncertainty of entrepreneurship. As you ponder your next steps, consider these questions to help navigate through the unknown:

1. Is there a dream you have been postponing? What is one small step you can take towards it today?
2. How can you create quiet moments for introspection each day?
3. What fears are holding you back?
4. Can you introduce brief pauses into your daily routine for better clarity?

5. How can your moments of reflection better align with your deepest values?

Here is where I leave you with a though - embrace pauses, embrace change, and embrace the unknown.

Through intentional reflection, discover your passions, face challenges head-on, and actively shape the life you want. Remember, recognizing your dreams is just the start. As we flip to the next chapter, we move from contemplation to action—where dreams begin to take shape in reality. So, take a deep breath, and let us boldly step into this journey of bringing our dreams to life. There is a world of excitement, challenges, and transformations waiting for us. Let us not just dream about the life we want but actively live it.

CHAPTER 6

GROWTH BEYOND THE GRIND

Implementing Changes and Taking First Steps

Facing the fear and uncertainty that comes with new ventures is daunting, but it is within these challenges that we find the greatest growth opportunities. Embracing uncertainty is the first step towards new beginnings, filled with the energy and excitement of pursuing what we love.

The concept of taking an intentional pause was a game-changer for me, particularly in transitioning from the corporate world to entrepreneurship. It prompted a myriad of questions about the need for a pause, its benefits, my strengths, and what brings me joy. Introducing intentional pauses into my life opened up a new realm of possibilities. An intentional pause acts like a "reset" button, providing a moment to realign our focus, reflect, and redirect our efforts toward what truly matters. It is not just about finding free time, but about utilizing that time effectively, with a clear plan and purpose in mind.

Tapping into what makes us tick, it is all about diving deep into who we are. Think of it as setting off on a quest right into the heart of what you are all about—your dreams, talents, and what gets you fired up. By giving ourselves the space to just be, through intentional pauses, we open doors to self-discovery, peeling back the layers to reveal our true potential and setting the stage for both personal and professional growth.

So here is a glimpse into my own journey of transformation, my evolution into Effie 2.0! It was clear to me that carving out time for thoughtful reflection was essential. Picture this: me, on my front porch, coffee in hand, surrounded by the calm of nature. That quiet moment was transformative, slowing down the chaos in my mind and bringing clarity.

With a fresh perspective, I was eager to dive deeper into my strengths and passions, but I wanted insights beyond just my own. I decided to send out a survey to friends, family, clients, and colleagues—a mix of people who could offer diverse viewpoints. This was not just about self-affirmation; it was about aligning my self-perception with the external world as I ventured into entrepreneurship. If their views matched mine, great; if not, it was time for some introspection.

Here is the thing—our strengths are like our superpowers, energizing and driving us. I believe in focusing on these powers, making them even stronger, rather than fixating on weaknesses. By concentrating on what we excel at, we amplify our true selves, which resonates more authentically with those around us.

The survey turned out to be an eye-opener. I reached out to a broad spectrum of 40 people, getting responses via text, detailed emails, and heartfelt messages. The effort they put into their feedback was incredible. My journal, my trusty sidekick through it all, captured every insight, tallying up the common themes with good old-fashioned tick marks. And guess what? The consensus highlighted my knack for connecting with others—a validating and heartwarming revelation that confirmed I was on the right path with my business venture. It was a crucial piece of the puzzle, affirming my journey towards the most authentic version of myself, Effie 2.0. This clarity and encouragement powered me through the ups and downs of building my business, fueling my passion and perseverance.

The GROWTH Strategy

How about kicking off with a spark of inspiration from a car ad that hit home with its "Start Your Impossible" challenge. It boils down to a simple truth: you do not have to be extraordinary to begin, but you need to begin to become extraordinary. That first step? It is everything.

"Because you don't NEED to be amazing to start. But you NEED to start to be amazing" (Millers, 2021). So, it is time to embark on our journey of GROWTH, filled with purposeful goal setting and crafting a personalized roadmap to success. This chapter is not just a narrative; it is an interactive guide designed to walk you through each step, with encouragement and support.

The **GROWTH Strategy** is a holistic approach to setting and achieving meaningful goals, starting with:

❖ **G**et in Tune: Kick off with some self-reflection. What sets your soul on fire? Is it helping others, unleashing your creativity, or perhaps, diving into new adventures? Pinpoint your strengths and dream big about your personal and professional life. What is your definition of success? Nail down what you are passionate about and let that shape your mission and legacy.

❖ **R**ecord Your Insights: Use your journal not just as a tool for recording daily events, but as a reflective space to discover patterns and dreams that might have been overlooked. This practice can illuminate your true passions, guiding you toward your calling.

❖ **O**rganize Your Priorities: Align your daily actions with your larger aspirations. If your family comes first, aim for a flexible career. Driven by innovation? Chase roles that spark your creative genius.

❖ **W**ork on Smaller Steps: Break your goals into bite-sized pieces. Dreaming of starting a nonprofit? Start with research, then volunteer, and move on to drafting a plan. Each small step is crucial and transformative, much like a caterpillar's journey to becoming a butterfly.

❖ **T**rack Your Progress: Regularly assess your journey towards your goals. Celebrate each small victory and learn from each challenge. This continuous evaluation keeps you motivated and on track.

❖ **H**ighlight Your Success: Take time to celebrate every achievement, big or small. Each milestone is a testament to your persistence and a step closer to realizing your full potential.

The journey of a butterfly, from cocoon to flight, mirrors our paths of growth and transformation. For me, butterflies hold a special place, symbolizing change, hope, and a tender connection to Madi. They remind me of the beauty and strength in transformation, encouraging me to embrace change with courage and grace.

55

Just like the butterfly, you possess the resilience to navigate life's shifts and emerge anew. Remember, each step in your GROWTH journey is an opportunity to spread your wings and soar toward your dreams with courage and grace. So, let us embrace this adventure with open hearts and minds, ready to discover the strength and beauty within.

Choices That Define Us: Decision-Making and Steering Life's Journey

Let us take a moment for a real talk about the crossroads we have all faced. Making those big, life-altering decisions can feel like standing at a crossroads, each path a testament to who we are or might become. These moments are not just about choosing; they are about discovering ourselves, challenging our fears, and sometimes, embracing the courage to shift directions. It is crucial to remember that it is perfectly fine to change your mind. The beauty of life lies in its fluidity, where few things are truly set in stone.

Reflecting on my own pivotal decision to transition from the structured world of finance to the vibrant landscape of entrepreneurship, I recognize the common thread that binds us all: the dance between the security of the familiar and the allure of the unknown. My journal, my BFF, a silent witness to the inner turmoil and triumphs of this journey, became a sanctuary, a place to confront and embrace my 'whys'—those deep-seated reasons propelling me forward.

Have you ever revisited your decisions, to reassure yourself that you are on the right path?

56

Deciding to forge my path was filled with second-guessing, but I found clarity and reassurance in the quiet moments of reflection. Those pauses for introspection reminded me of what I was leaving behind and what I hoped to discover ahead. Each reflection renewed my excitement for the future.

Belief in oneself is crucial on this journey. While stumbling may occur, maintaining faith in one's choices can significantly influence their path. For me, walks for clarity were essential times when I could step back, breathe, and ensure my decisions aligned with my true essence and aspirations.

I encourage you to reflect on your journey. What decisions have defined you? How do you maneuver through the uncertainties and doubts? Together, let us explore how our choices, big or small, shape the course of our lives and align us with our authentic selves.

Pilot Projects as Pathways to Change

When embarking on the entrepreneurial path, I faced a crucial decision: to cautiously test my business ideas before fully committing. This led me to the concept of pilot projects, my experimental playgrounds where I could validate the viability of my ventures amidst the demands of my finance career. After office hours, I would shift focus to these projects, driven by the sheer passion and determination to bring my dream to fruition.

This phase of my journey marked a transition from the predictability of finance to the uncharted landscapes of entrepreneurship. It was a tale of cautious exploration, where I embraced the challenge of venturing into new territories while still anchored in my professional role. I reached out to familiar nonprofits and companies with a proposition to offer my services pro bono. This strategy was not about undervaluing my work but rather laying the foundation for a greater vision, a test to see if my ideas could resonate and make an impact.

Now, you might wonder, "What if I am not aiming to start a business?" The beauty of pilot projects lies in their versatility. Whether you're considering a new hobby or a lifestyle change, these small-scale experiments allow you to test the waters. It is about starting with manageable initiatives, like organizing a weekend event related to your new interest or volunteering in a field you are curious about.

A practical tip: Engage your network. Solicit feedback from friends, family, or colleagues to participate in your pilot project. Their feedback can offer fresh perspectives and insights, acting as a personal focus group to refine your ideas.

This approach significantly shifted my perspective. It bolstered my confidence, allowing me to make well-informed decisions and realize the power of starting small. Every monumental dream begins with a modest step. So, whether you are plotting to launch a business or simply exploring a newfound interest, remember that it is the incremental steps that lay the groundwork for substantial achievements. What minor action can you undertake today to edge closer to your dreams?

Reflect on the resources and individuals in your sphere who might help bring your ideas to life. Remember, the essence lies not in executing a flawless leap, but in making that initial, deliberate move.

Diving into my pilot projects underscored the invaluable role of external feedback. This led to a pivotal moment in my journey—seeking assistance.

When I began my venture on this entrepreneurial path, I acknowledged the necessity of not going at it alone. Hence, I took a somewhat daunting step—requesting help. I contacted a broad spectrum of individuals, not only those within my close circle but also those who could offer distinct viewpoints. It was akin to unveiling a room filled with varied mirrors, each offering a distinct view of my path.

The prospect of asking for advice stirred a whirlwind of emotions within me. Doubts like, "Will they think I am an indecisive person?" or "What if their feedback contradicts my plans?" crept in. Yes, showing this vulnerability was challenging, riddled with self-doubt and fears of seeming inadequate. I grappled with fears of appearing less competent or confident. However, it is through embracing these moments of hesitancy that our most significant growth occurs.

These dialogues, characterized by genuine openness, transcended mere affirmation. The feedback received, though at times challenging to accept, provided an essential perspective shift, akin to viewing my project through a new lens. The journey was punctuated with revelations and guidance that prompted unexpected directions, some discussions energized me, while others prompted thoughtful reconsideration. Each interaction proved invaluable.

For those contemplating a pivot, and feeling tentative and uncertain, I encourage you to seek out support. Embrace the complex beauty of seeking support. It is not an admission of weakness but a testament to your strength and willingness to evolve. It is an acknowledgment that the collective insight and experience of others can enrich and refine your vision.

Your openness to assistance not only signifies your readiness for growth but also transforms your perceived vulnerabilities into strengths. The collective wisdom of your network becomes a crucial support system. So, make that call, send that message, and you will be astonished at the opportunities that unfold with the simple act of seeking assistance.

Strategic Solitude

As I progressed, the wisdom gleaned from reaching out for help naturally led me to embrace the solitude of a personal retreat. This was not merely about taking a break; it was a deliberate act of creating space for my ideas to breathe and grow.

Imagine embarking on something truly transformative—the personal retreat. Simple in concept yet profoundly impactful, a personal retreat became my sanctuary during a pivotal pause. It was an opportunity to step away from the frenetic pace of daily life and immerse myself in deep reflection and strategic planning. This dedicated time allowed me to focus intensely on my aspirations, crafting the blueprint for my entrepreneurial vision in a setting free from distractions.

Personal retreats transformed my usual vacation days into dedicated periods for nurturing my dreams and goals. These retreats did not necessitate exotic locales but were about finding a space resonating with my spirit, whether a sunlit nook at home, a local café, or a park bench amidst tranquility. The goal was to forge a haven for undisturbed thought, a retreat where my ideas could unfold and thrive.

These retreats plunged me into the depths of planning for my business. Armed with just my journal and a surge of creativity, I ventured into every possibility, shaping the future of my enterprise. A personal retreat gifts your future self by allowing you to untangle your thoughts, breathe life into your ideas, and hear the directives of your heart clearly, guiding you toward your true north.

You do not need to wait for the perfect moment to start. Begin where you are, with the resources at your disposal. Your retreat can be modest or grand, but the essential element is your dedication to your dreams.

Consider setting aside time for yourself and your aspirations. Allow yourself the luxury of uninterrupted thought, and the freedom to explore your desires and plans in depth. You might find that clarity and inspiration emerge from these quiet moments of solitude.

Transitioning from finance to entrepreneurship reshaped my everyday life, underscoring the importance of time management and prioritization. This journey illuminated the vitality of dedicating energy to my passions, proving that when a dream is truly valued, time can always be found to nurture it, no matter the existing commitments.

Through the process, there were moments of self-doubt, yet these experiences underscored the essence of my transition to entrepreneurship: it is about embarking on new paths, seeking guidance, allowing for reflection, and welcoming change. These principles apply not only to career transitions but also to life's broader spectrum, offering a roadmap for new hobbies or significant life changes.

Let us now pivot and engage our minds. With your *"Power of the Pause Journal"* in hand, embark on an exploratory quest. Ready to delve, reflect, and perhaps unveil new facets of yourself? Proceed!

Identify your pilot project. Is it a career shift, a hobby, or a wellness goal?

1. Who in your circle could offer invaluable advice or encouragement? Who is that person in your life?
2. Ever thought of dedicating a day off to a creative planning or brainstorming session? Envision that scenario.
3. Reflect on a significant decision you made recently. What did it teach you?
4. Do your daily actions and choices align with your long-term ambitions?
5. What is one action you plan to take next in your project or goal?

Happy journaling, and may this process illuminate your path as brightly as your dreams.

PART 3

UNEXPECTED AND UNWANTED PAUSES

NAVIGATING LOSS

CHAPTER 7

CONFRONTING LIFE'S UNEXPECTED TWISTS

When life throws the unexpected at you—those moments you never choose – that is when the *"Power of the Pause"* becomes crucial. March 4th, 2021 was a day like any other until it wasn't. It was a beautiful morning, and I was imbued with an unusual sense of joy. A casual walk and a chat with a friend set the tone for a promising day. That evening, as I settled in and passed by our family photos, Madison's smile in one caught my attention, and a strange feeling washed over me, like a sudden drop on a rollercoaster, an inexplicable sensation gripped my stomach - maybe an unconscious premonition of the heartbreaking news that was about to unfold.

The moment that every parent fears struck with merciless precision. Two police officers stood at our door that evening, their arrival alone was a harbinger of tragedy. The news they delivered shattered my world into unrecognizable fragments. My beloved 19-year-old daughter, Madison, had been in a car accident and had not survived. Time ceased in that instant. Their words, 'She did not make it,' felt like a physical blow, leaving me reeling in disbelief. The phrase lingered in the air. I was in denial, 'This cannot be Madison,' I thought, unable to reconcile with what my heart already understood. The shock of losing Madison, the sheer impossibility of it, rendered everything unreal. Unable to believe it was her. My mind rebelled against the reality, denying the possibility that it could be my vibrant, lively Madison involved in such a calamity.

After their departure, a profound silence engulfed the house, a stillness so intense it felt almost tangible. Their words echoed in my mind, yet comprehension eluded me. The world blurred into a haze of shock and disbelief. The reality of losing Madison, my radiant girl brimming with life, seemed an unthinkable anomaly. I found myself in a distorted reality, where nothing aligned and everything familiar was inverted. That night, which began so ordinarily, marked the beginning of a new, uncharted journey.

In retrospect, the unease I felt that morning seems like the first of many profound, albeit unknowing, connections I would continue to share with Madison, even in her absence. A bond that endures, palpable and unbroken, to this day.

After the officers left with the heart-wrenching news, my mother, living in our attached in-law suite, rushed over, her expression revealing her immediate concern, a mirror to the gravity of the situation we had just been thrust into. She tried her best to console me, her arms reaching out in a desperate attempt to provide some semblance of comfort amidst the shock. But I was in so much shock; I found myself unable to even embrace her. Her hugs, usually a source of solace, felt distant as I grappled with the reality of what we had just learned. This moment encapsulated the overwhelming nature of such profound grief, where even the most earnest attempts at consolation can feel disconnected from the whirlwind of emotions one is experiencing.

Picking up my phone to call and inform Athena, Madison's sister, was an exceedingly challenging task. Finding the right words to convey such devastating news seemed nearly impossible, as my voice, choked with tears, struggled to articulate the unimaginable. Upon hearing the news, Athena was struck with shock and profound sorrow, her reality becoming unrecognizable. Driven by an instinctive need to be close in this moment of heartache, her first impulse was to rush home. However, out of concern for her safety on the roads, heightened by the recent tragedy of Madi's accident, I insisted she wait until morning. Despite my deep longing for her presence, the fear of her traveling amidst such emotional turmoil was too significant to ignore.

Lester, my rock, somehow managed to hold himself together despite his own shock and trauma, a testament to his strength and love. He took care of me, even as he grappled with his own overwhelming emotions. When I found myself unable to gather my senses, overwhelmed by grief, it was Lester who steadied me. He took me to the ER in the middle of the night, a necessary step as I struggled to process the unfathomable loss. His presence and actions during this time were not just acts of support but also of immense personal fortitude, facing his own anguish while ensuring my safety and well-being.

The scene in the triage is vivid in my memory. I could not articulate my pain to the nurse, the words lost amidst my sobs. An uncanny coincidence struck me as the ER room number, 21, mirrored the time of Madi's birth, 9:21 a.m. It felt like a subtle connection to Madi amidst the chaos.

A compassionate nurse, whose name I regretfully cannot recall, sat by me, holding my hands and looking into my eyes for what felt like hours, with empathy that seemed to resonate with my soul. She, too, a mother of a 19-year-old girl, softly expressed her sorrow, her words "I am so, so sorry," echoing my own heartache. Despite their efforts to soothe me, the desire to escape this harrowing reality persisted.

The return home, supported by that kind nurse and Lester's steady presence, remains a blur. The day unfolded in a whirlwind, making each moment indistinct and fleeting. As we arrived, friends like Stacey and Michele gathered, offering shoulders to cry on. Their presence was a comfort, yet the overwhelming nature of the day meant that everything seemed to merged into a blur, with moments passing by like shadows, each one indistinguishable from the next in the fog of grief. Amidst my tears, I repeated, "I don't want a funeral, I don't want to hear apologies, I don't want any of this..." — a mantra of denial and grief.

As I sit here, translating my memories into words, I am transported back to that whirlwind of emotions, to that night when my world shattered. The days that followed were a blend of heartache and numbness. People came and went, offering comforting words, but it all felt like distant noise compared to the silent scream inside me. The thought that Madison, my girl with her bright smile, big blue eyes, and boundless heart, would never walk through our door again was inconceivable.

In those early days, I was engulfed in a world of pain. Every attempt at comfort from others seemed futile. My mind constantly replayed memories of Madison – her laughter, her dreams, our plans. It felt like being trapped in a never-ending nightmare. I found myself lost in memories, in "what ifs" and "if onlys". Every corner of our home, every song, every shared moment, reminded me of her. The sense of emptiness was all-consuming. I would sit in Madison's room, surrounded by her belongings, trying desperately to feel her presence, to bridge the gap between us. My heart ached with a pain I had never known before. A part of me left with her. Waking up each day to her absence was an ordeal. Every morning, I hoped it was all just a bad dream, only to be hit by the brutal reality again. I was thrust into a new, unwanted reality where Madison would never walk through our door again—a reality I could not, and still cannot, accept.

Our culture struggles to understand how to truly pause with grief. We are not taught how to support someone who has lost a loved one, especially a loss as unnatural as losing a child. It feels so wrong, so unfair, to have to say goodbye to your child before you.

A Journey Through Loss

Life can be brutal, presenting you with the shittiest unimaginable challenges. People often ask me, "Effie, how do you find the strength to face each day?" Some try to empathize, saying things like, "I can only imagine," or "I cannot even begin to imagine." Others attempt to find reason in it, labeling it as "God's plan." And then there are those who remain silent, perhaps because the grief is too close to their own fears, or they think what happened to me could happen to them too.

But the hard truth is, grief is an inescapable part of life. It is one of those forces beyond our control, no matter how much we wish otherwise. One of the most hurtful things someone said to me was:

"God sacrificed Madison to save other children".

Can you believe that? Such words not only made me angry at the person who said them but also at the world at large.

I believe grief is so terrifying that it makes people run away. When they flee from grief, they also flee from you. I was lucky to have my family and close friends—those I consider my true family—stay by my side. However, I was astounded by the number of people who just vanished. I understand that grief is daunting, but feeling abandoned is the last thing anyone needs when engulfed in such deep sorrow. This journey is already incredibly lonely.

This experience has been a revelation in many ways. It has shown me the immense power of grief, the fear it instigates, and how it can either draw people closer or push them away. Throughout all this, I have learned to appreciate those who remained, those unafraid to sit with me in my pain. These are the people who truly grasp the essence of love and support.

As I write, I am still navigating through grief and healing. This path is indefinite, a process of learning to live in a world without Madison. Every day, I carry her in my heart, seeking ways to honor her memory and keep her spirit vibrant. It is about taking small steps, finding peace amidst sorrow, and gradually rebuilding. This chapter of my life is still ongoing, a path I did not choose but am learning to walk, always with Madison in my heart and memories.

Subsequently, we will explore how to genuinely support someone grieving, particularly parents who have lost a child. The insights I share are from my heart, reflecting my experiences. This next phase is more than my story; it is an opportunity for collective growth and a re-examination of how we deal with grief. We will journey through this together, embracing the lessons in compassion and understanding that lie ahead.

True resilience is not about avoiding pain; it is about living with it and transforming it into growth. Together, we will navigate life's challenges, drawing strength from our shared stories and the quiet resilience that sustains us in the toughest times.

From Lemons to Legacy - Finding Purpose in the Unexpected

You might be curious about my perspective on lemons. There is a well-known saying "when life gives you lemons, make lemonade" (Johnen, 2016). However, I have always believed that sometimes, the lemons life gives you are so sour that lemonade just does not suffice. So, here is my approach: "When life gives you lemons, throw them as hard as you can!" That is right - take those whole lemons, sliced ones, any kind, and throw them at the sky, the wall, the ground—hurl them with all your might!

For me, throwing lemons became a form of therapy. There was a day when I was overflowing with anger—furious at the world, at God, frustrated by the sheer unfairness of everything, and deeply upset that Madi was no longer with us. My anxiety was off the charts, a level I had never experienced before. So, I thought, "Effie, since you have never punched anyone (yet!), why not throw some lemons?" Madison adored lemons—she would take them from our drinks and simply enjoy them. This inspired me to grab a bunch of lemons, slice them up, and start hurling them against the brick wall in our backyard. Believe me, it felt incredibly liberating.

I even involved Lester, my mother, Athena, and a few friends. It became our thing – releasing all that frustration, one lemon at a time. It might sound strange, but it is effective. It provides a way to release all the anger, sadness, and anxiety physically and tangibly.

Madison's own words from her journal hit me like a wave every time I read them. She wrote:

> *"My Dream: To help people and be famous in any type of way. Everyone in the US knows who Madison Ebie is. Famous attorney, CSI job, or anything to be known in a positive way. I am Madi of Tampa, FL I am ridiculously passionate about becoming something famous & important to help people— because I can serve society more positively. I don't have it all together, but I have a plan & I will change the WORLD!"*

Her spirit just leaps off the page, doesn't it?

The Effie Santos TEDx Talk – Westshore

The morning of my TEDx talk, I woke up at the crack of dawn, around 5:00 a.m. This was a day charged with anticipation and a deep need for reflection. In those quiet early hours, I sought a moment of solitude to connect with Madison's spirit, seeking her strength to guide me through the day. I rehearsed my speech meticulously, each word and pause carefully considered, amidst a blend of excitement and anxiety. This day was not just about delivering a talk; it was my first major public appearance since Madison's tragic accident, and it felt like a reunion with friends, colleagues, and business partners.

As Lester and I drove to the venue, he, ever the optimist, tried lifting my spirits by playing "I Look Good Today" by O.T. Genasis on the radio, but I craved silence and stillness to center my thoughts. Arriving at the venue, a surge of emotions hit me as people greeted me with warmth and condolences for Madison. Overwhelmed, Lester and I retreated to a secluded room near the stage, which became my sanctuary, a place to focus and gather my strength, a place where I had to remind myself to breathe and stay present. I practiced my speech, every word, every pause, and as the moment for me to speak was approaching, I suddenly felt a wave of panic. "Have I forgotten my lines?" I wondered to myself. In a quiet, reassuring whisper, almost like a pep talk, I murmured, "Effie, you've got this. Madi, I need you more than ever, right here by my side." It was a moment of seeking inner strength and calling upon Madison's spirit for support.

Walking onto that stage felt like crossing into a new chapter from my old corporate world to starting fresh as an entrepreneur. I was there, heart full, ready to share not just my story but also the dreams Madi once penned down. Lester and Athena, their hands clasped together, in a mix of nervous anticipation and support, bolstered my courage. They were my silent cheerleaders amidst all those watching eyes.

I talked about the ups and downs, the doubts, and the wins that came with choosing a path less traveled. It wasn't just my adventure; it was about the lessons learned, the growth that came from every challenge. The narrative seamlessly transitioned to Madi. With my head high, I cradled her journal, her words ready to be voiced aloud. It was more than reading her words; we did not just pay tribute; we forged a deep connection, intertwining her dreams with the collective ambitions of all who listened. With her picture beside me, shining bright, I shared her hopes and dreams, turning the page for everyone to see. It was more than my journey; it was about the strength found in pauses, in quiet moments before big leaps, and in the courage to share our stories, weaving together our dreams and aspirations.

That moment, Madison transcended being my daughter; she became a memory for everyone present. A significant milestone as we neared the first anniversary of her passing. It was my way of ensuring that the world remembers Madison Ebie, just as she dreamed.

The response to my TEDx talk was overwhelming. As I received a standing ovation, a chant started in the crowd, growing louder: "Madison." Hearing her name echo through the room brought tears to my eyes, a testament to her enduring impact. The support for Madi's foundation and the empathetic apologies from those unsure of what to say previously, touched my heart.

The day concluded with a heartwarming gathering at my dear friend Kristen's home, an 'after-party' that served as a beautiful closure to an emotionally charged day. Surrounded by those closest to me, including Kristen who has been a pillar of support, the warmth and camaraderie of the evening were a testament to the love and strength that encircle me. It was a fitting way to honor Madison's memory, reminding me of the unbreakable bonds of friendship and the beautiful circle of support that surrounds us.

Today, each time I read Madi's journal, feeling her ambition and hope, it solidifies my resolve. I was inspired to not only chase Madi's dreams but to bring them to life. Creating a nonprofit in her spirit, her drive, and her wish to make a difference was my next step. Now, I am fulfilling this mission – working in spirit with Madison to effect change, to impact the world as she aspired. We are doing this together, her legacy and dreams guiding every step.

The Legacy: Honoring Madison

Madi's Movement, inspired by Madison's own aspirations, is a nonprofit dedicated to supporting foster teens in achieving independence and success. Collaborating with businesses and communities, our focus is on preparing these youths for real-world challenges by enhancing their education, job skills, and personal development. The aim is to equip every teenager aging out of foster care with the necessary tools for life, ensuring they can fully realize their potential.

More than just assistance, Madi's Movement is committed to ensuring these teens thrive. Through various programs and workshops like "Financial Foundations", "SuperSkills Academy", "Empowered Education", and "Career Connections", alongside mentorship and essential resources, we provide a crucial support system as they transition into adulthood.

Empowerment is at the heart of Madi's Movement. Our goal is for these teens to understand that they can pursue their dreams, forge successful paths, and make a tangible difference in the world. This initiative is a continuation of Madison's legacy— one of positivity, aid, and significant impact. Each step in Madi's Movement propels us towards a future where these teens can confidently face life's challenges. To learn more, engage, or support, visit Madi's Movement website www.madismovement.org.

Legacy, however, isn't only about grand gestures or starting movements. It is woven into the fabric of our daily lives – be it through continuing loved ones' traditions, sharing their stories, or small acts of kindness inspired by them. It is about keeping their spirit alive in your actions, values, and supported causes. This could manifest as volunteering in their favorite field, pursuing a hobby they cherished, or living by the lessons they imparted. Every action reflecting their influence on your life contributes to their enduring legacy.

As we each move through our own paths of grief and healing, it is important to remember the strength we possess to transform our sorrow into something that honors those we have lost. This can be through initiatives like "Madi's Movement" or simple daily acts that showcase their influence on us. We all have the capacity to forge and live out meaningful legacies.

The essence of this journey, whether it is a foreseeable pause or an unexpected halt, is to allow ourselves time to reflect, grieve, and find our way. One's experience may vary, but challenges are a universal aspect of life. The manner in which these challenges are approached and overcome shapes an individual's journey.

Do we let these challenges overwhelm us, or do we use them to create something positive?

In my experience, these challenges—both real and symbolic—have become emblems of resilience. They represent turning life's hardships into something purposeful and healing. It is about acknowledging the pain, the grief, and the anger, and channeling these emotions into honoring our loved ones and our personal growth.

So, let us embrace the lemons of life, the challenges, the unexpected breaks in our journey, and navigate through the tough times together—with a little bit of sourness mix, resilience and heartfelt determination.

CHAPTER 8

THE HEALING PATH

Gathering Strength

In life's journey, pauses are essential. They are moments for self-kindness, for giving ourselves the space we need. It is about authenticity, living true to our essence without concern for the opinions or judgments of others. I acknowledge that this is challenging. It requires a daily, conscious effort.

When life presents unexpected pauses, my advice is to fully embrace them. Understand them completely. These pauses do not follow a set of rules or a checklist. They are unique experiences and navigating them is a personal journey. These moments are not just interruptions; they are integral parts of your life's journey, providing opportunities for reflection, regrouping, and rediscovery.

My journey has taught me the importance of consistency and compassion. The support of friends and family has been invaluable. The simple acts of reaching out, the reminders of being loved, and the willingness to listen without trying to fix everything have been crucial. Grief is a lingering presence that evolves and becomes part of your identity, requiring time and space to be acknowledged.

Taking this pause was necessary for me. It has been a space to grieve, to cherish Madison's memories, and to understand my own transformations. I am still in the midst of this journey, evolving into a new yet familiar version of myself—a different kind of mother, wife, daughter, and friend.

Finding Hope

The recurring question in my mind is, "What does my life look like now after losing Madison?" It is a tough journey, and I am still searching for answers. There is a constant ache, but it is through this pain that I am learning and growing. During this pause, I am discovering new ways to feel connected to Madi. It feels like we have a unique language that transcends words. I am more attuned to the signs she sends, each one a gentle nudge reminding me she is still part of my life.

I am learning to stay anchored in the present, avoiding the trap of 'what ifs' or dwelling on the past. It is a daily practice of facing this new reality, moment by moment. An important aspect of this journey is keeping Madison's spirit alive. I make sure her name is spoken, her memory cherished and celebrated.

This pause is a period of profound learning. It is teaching me to balance holding on and letting go, recognizing that grief and love are intertwined. I am embracing a new version of life, one where Madison's presence is felt differently, yet profoundly.

In moments of deep loss, it is common to hear people say, "Take as long as you need," acknowledging that grief does not adhere to a timetable. Yet, often in other areas of life, this understanding seems to fade, and there is an expectation to quickly recover, to move on as though our lives were not profoundly affected. But from each pause life has given me, I have learned something crucial: every interruption teaches you something valuable.

Remember, healing has no time limit. I frequently remind myself of this. We all progress on our individual journeys. Some days, it might feel like progress, other days, a step back. But this is normal and part of the healing process. There is no need to rush or meet a deadline when mending a heart.

I constantly remind myself, and I want to remind you too—it is alright to take your time. Allow yourself to feel and heal at your own pace. Do not let anyone rush you through your grief or growth. Each pause, each reflective moment, is part of your story, shaping you in ways you may not yet realize. So, take the time you need. There is no correct or incorrect way to navigate this journey. Just keep moving at the pace that is right for you.

A suggestion from my friend Helen to get a puppy turned out to be incredibly healing for me. The thought of getting a puppy initially seemed daunting, but welcoming Lucy, my cockapoo, into my life has been a significant step in moving forward. I sought a puppy that embodied Madison's spirit—sweet yet sassy, with a fearless voice, just like Madi.

When Lucy entered my life, it felt like a part of Madison's spirit came along with her. Lucy's vibrant eyes, her excited tail wagging, and her playful barks seemed to understand her special role in my healing. Caring for Lucy, with all the walks, feedings, and play, brought structure and joy back into my daily routine, giving me a reason to rise each morning and a comforting presence during quiet nights. Lucy intuitively knows when I need extra love. She curls up beside me on tough days or gently nudges me, as if to remind me that joy still exists. In those moments with Lucy, I feel a connection to Madison, a reminder of the love and energy she brought to our lives.

The happiness and laughter Lucy brings to our home are invaluable. She represents a living reminder that joy and love can coexist with sorrow. Lucy, in her own way, is aiding my healing process, reflecting the perfect balance of sweetness and sass – reminiscent of Madi.

Healing A Broken Heart

Taking a step that my therapist suggested, I began sharing my journey with a close circle of friends, creating a safe and intimate space for healing. This became a place where I could express myself openly and honestly. On January 10, 2022, I shared my raw and unfiltered thoughts with this trusted group. This is a direct window into my heart and mind from that day:

*** *** ***

"January 10, 2022

My Raw feelings during this unwanted journey - Unfiltered

As I sit in the dark...down in that deep hole...and each day my body feels like a tornado is inside...spinning around, twisted up...of every emotion and so much sadness and grief...I feel like

I am going to explode. So many new feelings and emotions…I think how can there be more? Really? The holidays took a toll on me physically and emotionally. When I get in this deep dark hole I isolate myself…I work hard not to but it's all I can do to just breathe and get through the day. My therapist thought it would be helpful and therapeutic to share my journey and feelings…here…in Madison's Love…with Madison and each of you that have stayed with me - my support system. I don't like talking about myself - I never want to feel like a burden or be negative- I sometimes feel people are tired of hearing me, hearing this…but this…44 weeks ago… seems like today. I replay it in my head over and over. I could never imagine that our bodies could endure so much pain, sadness and suffering. Before Madi's accident when I heard of a child passing, I use to think - oh my gosh I can't even imagine that I never want to imagine that the odds are so small it wouldn't happen to me or my family. I don't want to believe that it did happen…to Madi…to me…to our family…I can't…I am not ready for that…I look at Madi's pictures, videos, her saved voice mail to me and it's like how is this possible…this is a bad nightmare…Madi will be home soon, walking through the door, saying "hi mom, hi Lester"…giving us a hug and kiss, washing her hands, complaining about work and asking what's there to eat. She will be home late from work and come in our bedroom and give me a kiss and say good night mom good night Lester…I hold on to this for now. I cannot accept anything else right now. Some people say I can only imagine your pain…no you can't…I thought I could imagine the pain too...but you can't...the pain and sadness are like being in another galaxy another world...no one can imagine it unless it happens to you. Helen can imagine it, she is going through this journey, 4 years ago losing her beautiful daughter Logan at 20 years old...we lost Logan and Madi the same way. I am beyond blessed to have been connected to Helen and become great friends out of all of this heartache. She shares and shows me hope and the one that gets just as excited as I do when we receive signs from our beautiful daughters... knowing and feeling Madi and Logan are together...the girls have so many similarities and so many synchronicities it's truly amazing. Madi and Logan are teaching us and guiding us - to continue with their goals and dreams of making this world better.

I am a nurturing and worrying person- it's in my DNA...it's always been hard putting myself first...my girls have always been first...I love being a mom. It's a work in progress for sure...taking the time for me, breathing, mediating, yoga, feeling the heat on my body, getting therapy, spending time connecting with Madi, spending time with Athena, Lester, my mom, and our true supporters. It's really hard...I need to lean on my support more I just don't know what to ask for. As I work my way up to see the light at the opening of this dark hole...a work in progress - I still want to be the best mom to my girls, be the best wife to Lester and best daughter for my mom, be a good and supportive friend...it will just be a new me.

I needed to release this from my heart and mind".

***   ***   ***

Writing everything down, exposing my feelings in simple words, has been like a beam of light in this dark journey. It feels like slightly opening the curtains, allowing just enough brightness to guide my way. Sharing these experiences is not just a way to unload my feelings and emotions; it is about connecting with others on similar paths. We are in this together, each on our unique journey, yet finding commonality in our experiences. As I navigate through this blend of loss and love, I am slowly discovering a new version of myself. It is challenging, yet moments of clarity and strength emerge unexpectedly.

I have realized the significance of self-care, something I have often overlooked while caring for others. Now, I am learning to prioritize myself—to find time for quiet reflection, meditation, yoga, and simply enjoying the sunshine. Therapy has become a crucial part of my routine, along with nurturing connections with Madison, Athena, Lester, my mom, and relying on my support system. It is difficult, but immensely important. I aim to emerge from this period stronger and more whole, aspiring to be a better mother, wife, daughter, and friend.

Expressing these raw, unfiltered thoughts is my way of healing, learning about strength and hope, and navigating through sorrow. Each day brings more understanding of who I am in this new reality, where Madison is not physically present but still vividly part of my life. I am learning how to keep her memory warm and bright, guiding my path. This chapter, deeply intertwined with grief, is a testament to human resilience. It highlights finding hope and strength in the darkest times.

It is about discovering those sparks of light that remind us of the enduring beauty and love in life, guiding us onwards. In the profound sadness, I hold onto the belief that paths to healing and growth can be found.

CHAPTER 9

STANDING TOGETHER

Guiding Loved Ones Through the Shadows of Grief

Friends, grief is like life throwing the sourest lemon at you. I would like to take a moment to discuss how we can support those who are grieving, particularly parents who have endured the unimaginable loss of a child, as I have with Madison. As I mentioned earlier, I am not a licensed therapist; I am merely sharing from my own heartbreak and experiences. Grief is incredibly isolating, and the person suffering needs to feel less alone, not more. Grief is not just emotional; it affects the whole body. When you are deep in grief, well-intentioned questions like "What do you need?" or "What can I do for you?" can feel overwhelming. After Madison's accident, I found even simple gestures like a hug to be too much. This is why understanding the complexities of grief is vital.

Being there for someone who is grieving can be daunting. However, it is important not to let this fear distance you from them. It is a stark reminder that such a loss can happen to anyone, even to those we know. Sometimes, the best support you can offer is to acknowledge their pain. They need to sense your love and presence, to be reassured that you are there for them, steadfast in both good times and bad.

In terms of offering practical assistance, it is often the small, thoughtful actions that matter the most:

❖ Dropping off a meal or groceries without expecting a conversation can be incredibly helpful.

❖ Consider helping with everyday tasks like driving their children or assisting with household chores.

❖ It is important to remember that your support is about being there for them quietly and consistently, not about receiving gratitude or a reaction.

Grief can be paralyzing, so if the bereaved do not respond as you might expect, it is crucial not to take it personally. Continue sending those little messages of care, even if they go unanswered. The key is to be a steady presence, offering support without the expectation of immediate acknowledgment or gratitude.

On the emotional front, having patience is crucial. If you have not experienced a loss like this, you might not fully grasp what the grieving person is going through, and that is completely fine. Sometimes, simply saying…

"*I do not know what to say, but I am here for you*" is enough.

This shows acknowledgment of their pain and your willingness to support them in their difficult times. After I lost Madison, there were moments when I could not even bear to look at my phone, much less respond to messages. So, if a grieving friend or loved one seems distant or unresponsive, it is important to understand that it is not about you. They are just trying to find their way through immense pain.

Small gestures can be incredibly meaningful. Take my friend Sherri, for example. She regularly sends me cards every two weeks with light-hearted fun facts—nothing heavy, just something to bring a smile. It consistently brightens my day, reminding me she is thinking of me.

When checking in with someone grieving, consider asking—

"How are you right now?"

Recognizing that grief is a moment-to-moment journey is crucial. Since losing Madison, I have changed; it has been a difficult and transformative process. But it is important to remember that grief is not contagious. Being there for someone in their grief will not engulf you in darkness. At the same time, the small, continuous acts of kindness are what really count. These gestures can help someone find their way again in a world that has been turned upside down. Being present for someone, not just immediately after their loss but throughout the long and challenging journey of healing that follows, is invaluable. This combined approach acknowledges the changing nature of grief while emphasizing the importance of sustained support and kindness.

PART 4

THE GIFTS OF THE PAUSE

HARNESSING THE POWER

CHAPTER 10

STABLE GROUNDS

Adapting to New Realities

Change, indeed, is where we forge our resilience, where we gather the tools of courage that accompany us on the journey to new beginnings. The experience of venturing from the corporate realm into entrepreneurship was not just a career shift for me; it was the embodiment of taking a pause, a strategic halt I had not acknowledged until I was invited to share my journey at a TEDx event. That realization struck a chord—I had been intuitively crafting a path through my transition, embracing the excitement and the unknown with open arms.

This venture, while brimming with potential, was naturally accompanied by a spectrum of emotions, from exhilarating anticipation to the nuances of anxiety inherent in embracing the unfamiliar. The dynamism of stepping into a new role, preparing to meet the needs of new clients, encapsulated a delicate dance between eagerness and caution. It is essential to recognize that every fresh start, while promising, evokes a blend of feelings. Being 'new' in a field does not signify inexperience but rather brings a fresh perspective and vitality to the forefront, enriching our endeavors with innovation and passion.

Transitioning to new chapters in life is not solely about the positive shifts. The loss of my daughter, Madison, introduced a pause of a different nature, a profound and involuntary halt where existence narrowed down to moment-by-moment survival. Nearly three years on, the notion of 'adjustment' to life without her physical presence remains an elusive concept. Adjusting does not imply forgetting or moving on but learning to live with a reality that was never chosen.

Grief, with its complex and deeply personal path, fundamentally altered my existence. It is not about mere adjustment but about finding a way to continue living with a piece of one's heart perpetually absent. Grief morphs into a constant companion, its presence a testament to the depth of love and loss. In this journey, I have discovered the power of vulnerability, the catharsis in sharing our stories, and the strength in community. It is about growing with the pain, finding innovative ways to honor Madison's memory, and keeping her spirit vibrantly alive within me.

In these experiences lies a universal truth: change, whether sought or imposed, shapes us. It encourages us to embrace our vulnerabilities and draw strength from them. It invites us to share our stories, to connect with others on similar paths, and to find growth through our experiences.

Realities Of Navigating Loss and Embracing Transformation

Emerging from the shadows of grief is an intimate, personal journey that asks for patience and kindness towards oneself. It is a process of realizing that grief may not necessarily diminish; instead, we expand and grow around it, incorporating it into our new existence. It is not a matter of completing the grieving process because such a finish line does not exist. It is about learning to integrate our grief into our lives, allowing it to ebb and flow as naturally as the tides.

Rebuilding oneself after a loss is not a quick or easy journey. It requires therapy for some, the cultivation of a wellness support team for others, and the courage to face the stark reality of a new normal. It is a path where we must consciously decide to feel each emotion as it comes, it is about peeling away old layers and nurturing new growth in a process, often draining and transformative.

My therapist often reminds me, "Effie, what other choice do you have?" This question is not just for me; it is for all of us facing tough realities. We do not just adjust for ourselves; we do it for those we love. But the journey must start within us.

In confronting these harsh new realities, we may also confront the truths about our relationships. One of the toughest parts was realizing that not all friends could walk with me through the darkest times. It can be a sobering realization when we see that not everyone can journey with us through the darkest times. The loss of friendships, on top of personal loss, can compound the grief. However, it also clarifies who truly stands with us, it was like clearing the fog and seeing clearly; revealing the strength and authenticity of the relationships that withstand the test of tragedy.

Then there's the personal change that comes with loss. Facing the financial side of loss is tough. It is more than losing a paycheck – it is about what that paycheck means for our life and sense of security. It is when regular work can slide down the list, and money worries creep in. Yet, these moments also teach us invaluable lessons about being resourceful and highlight the importance of being financially prepared for unexpected turns in life.

Confronting the change within ourselves is equally vital. Recognizing and accepting that we have changed after a significant loss is part of the healing process. It is a profound shift, much like leaving a long-time career for a new venture. It is about growth and embracing a new version of us—richer in empathy, fortified in resilience, and deeper in understanding.

This is not merely about adapting to change; it is about growing from it, finding new strength in our vulnerabilities, and learning to view our experiences as steppingstones to a more empathetic and resilient self.

Life's rich pattern of experiences, both joyful and challenging, shapes us in profound ways. Adapting to new realities, whether they are changes we seek or those that are thrust upon us, requires a toolbox filled with courage, compassion, and an openness to the lessons that each experience brings. Each new reality presents an opportunity to grow, to learn, and to find new ways to thrive, armed with the wisdom of our past and the resilience for our future. This journey is about metamorphosis and finding the strength within to gracefully navigate the complexities life presents.

Embracing Change: The Journey of Adaptation and Growth

In confronting new phases of life, we often discover untapped potential and new pathways. Recognizing that the unfamiliar is not inherently negative opens us up to embrace innovation and vitality. Venturing beyond our usual confines can lead to personal enrichment and unanticipated opportunities.

Adjustment is an active journey—it begins with recognizing the shifts in our world, experiencing them fully, and then purposefully taking even the smallest steps toward acclimatization. It involves assembling an array of tools—like bravery and self-care—that empower us to manage change. Both exhilarating and painful alterations present chances for personal development and learning.

The role of a supportive network is invaluable as we adapt. As previously discussed, reaching out is a brave act, acknowledging our shared human experience. Assistance can come from professional counselors, friends, family, or community groups who empathize with our circumstances. Seeking such support is a sign of strength and a strategic approach to overcoming the hurdles that accompany change.

Reflection, too, is crucial. It enables us to digest the changes we encounter and find the inner fortitude often required to move forward.

With the insights gained, it is beneficial to take time with your thoughts, perhaps in your *"Power of the Pause Journal"*, to ponder the following questions. They are intended to guide you through your process of adapting to your new realities and recognizing the resilience within you.

1. What significant change have you recently faced, and how has it reshaped your daily life?
2. How have you personally responded to this new reality, both emotionally and practically?
3. What important lesson or insight have you gained while adapting to this change?
4. What has been your biggest challenge in this transition, and what success, however small, are you proud of?
5. Moving forward, what is one change you can make to better embrace future shifts in your reality?

Remember, you are not walking this path of change alone. We are all navigating our unique journeys, each of us finding our rhythm and pace. It is about granting yourself kindness and patience as you traverse this new landscape. By embracing this journey, you will discover an inner strength you might not have known existed.

Together, let us move forward, valuing the quiet moments that offer us insight and the inner fortitude to face life's shifts. It is more than merely enduring these transitions; it is about flourishing within them. Join hands with me and let us explore the richness that comes from welcoming new chapters in our lives.

CHAPTER 11

CREATING COLLECTIVE RESILIENCE

The Power of Your Lemon Community

Life certainly has a knack for hitting the pause button unexpectedly, doesn't it? When it does, instinct might tell us to bunker down solo, but here is a truth I have stumbled upon: inviting people into your world during these pauses is not just beneficial; it is essential. We are hardwired for connection, designed to share our highs, lows, and everything in between with others.

During my journey, I have leaned heavily into my circle of family and friends. They have been my rock, providing unwavering support and comfort reminiscent of a warm, hearty meal. Yet, my quest for connection did not end there. I ventured out, expanding my circle to what I have lovingly termed my 'Lemon Community.' These individuals, initially strangers to my path, brought with them fresh perspectives, new tales, and insights that challenged my thinking and enriched my journey.

Engaging with this diverse group was akin to flinging open the windows on the first warm day of spring, inviting a gust of fresh ideas and viewpoints that illuminated new facets of my life and challenges.

It is these interactions that have offered me alternative ways to perceive and navigate my journey, shedding light on aspects previously unseen.

And about that mantra from my TEDx talk about opting to throw lemons instead of succumbing to the cliché of making lemonade? That has been a guiding principle for me. Life's lemons, those unexpected and often unwelcome surprises, sometimes demand a response more cathartic than simply making the best of a sour situation. It is about channeling all that pent-up frustration, anger, and pain in a way that is not just constructive but therapeutic.

The essence of the Lemon Community embodies this principle. It is a gathering not just for back-patting and optimistic spin-doctoring. This community is about getting real with life's adversities, recognizing those moments when making lemonade is not on the agenda, and you just need to vent, to rage against the storm. And they are right there with you, ready to pitch in and throw their lemons into the fray.

As we delve into this chapter, let us remember the importance of curating your own Lemon Community. It is about surrounding yourself with folks who can handle life's full spectrum—the sweet moments and the inevitable sour ones. They are your squad for the lemonade-making days and your comrades when it is time to let loose and launch those lemons into oblivion. It is a commitment to facing life's unpredictable nature head-on, together.

Reflecting on my Lemon Community, I cherish the blend of long-standing friends who anchor me and the new connections that invigorate my journey. My leap into entrepreneurship, a significant 'lemon' in my life, illustrated the invaluable role this community played. The unwavering support from those who have been with me for years combined with the fresh insights from fellow entrepreneurs I met along the way provided a balanced blend of encouragement and enlightenment. They have shared in the triumphs and the trials, contributing zest to the bittersweet adventure of forging a new path.

This journey of intentional pause, of stepping boldly into the unknown to redefine my trajectory and tap into unexplored potentials, has been a profound learning curve. It has been about business, sure, but also about life, about discovering facets of myself I had not recognized before.

Solace and Strength in Shared Experiences

Life has its way of pressing pause, unexpectedly bringing us to moments we never anticipated. It is during these times that the value of community becomes undeniably clear. Not just any community, but one that truly understands the depth of our experiences—my 'Lemon Community.' This group formed not only of longstanding friends and family but also of individuals who, though once strangers, have become integral to navigating life's toughest challenges.

The loss of my daughter, Madison, was a moment that seemed to stop time itself. The familiar patterns of life suddenly became alien landscapes of grief, leaving me adrift in a sea of sorrow. It was then I realized the profound necessity of connection, not merely for solace but for shared understanding and support. My Lemon Community shone brightly in these darkest hours, offering guidance and presence when I felt most alone.

Joanne, a friend who reached out during this time, became a pivotal figure in this journey. Her own experience of losing her daughter created a bridge of empathy and understanding that words alone could not build. Our conversations, filled with the raw and real aspects of grief, offered a kind of solace and permission to grieve in my way. Joanne's presence marked the beginning of a transformative phase in my life, teaching me the importance of grieving on my terms and the necessity of self-care amid profound loss.

Then there is Tracey, whose connection took on new depth after Madison's accident. Her outreach and shared experience of losing her son, Craig, created a bond forged through mutual understanding of loss. Tracey's story, her resilience in the face of unimaginable grief, brought not only comfort but also a living example of enduring strength. She became an integral part of my support network, embodying the truth that while grief may be a constant companion, it does not solely define us.

These connections, these moments of shared understanding and support, have underscored the importance of the Lemon Community in my life. They have shown me that while grief can feel isolating, it does not have to be endured alone. There are others, like Joanne and Tracey, who have traversed this painful path, and who can stand with you and offer a hand in the darkest times.

This journey through grief and the formation of my Lemon Community has taught me invaluable lessons about the power of connection, the strength found in shared experiences, and the resilience that emerges from embracing both the sweet and the sour moments of life. It is a testament to the enduring human spirit, the capacity for growth in the face of loss, and the profound impact of community in our lives.

Connecting Hearts

Life's unexpected pauses often lead us into isolation, but it is in these moments that reaching out and creating connections becomes essential. Sharing the story of my daughter Madi's accident was incredibly difficult, especially during the isolating times of Covid-19. The decision to share our story on social media was both a release and a moment of profound vulnerability, leading to an outpouring of support that was both overwhelming and deeply comforting.

Among the sea of messages, Gina's stood out, offering a connection to Helen, another mother who had endured the incomprehensible loss of her daughter, Logan. Helen and I discovered an immediate bond through our shared grief, finding solace in the understanding and empathy that only those who have faced similar losses can offer. This was the beginning of a deeply meaningful bond, one that not only offered solace but also a shared understanding of our grief.

Our first conversation, filled with raw emotion and mutual understanding, marked the start of what I call my "Lemon Community." This unique support system, comprising both old friends and new ones, became a beacon of light in the darkest times. It wasn't just about finding people who could empathize with the loss but also about connecting with those who could embrace the entirety of the journey, including the moments when making lemonade from life's lemons was not an option.

Helen, in particular, became a mentor in navigating grief, offering insights and understanding that only someone who has walked this path could provide. Our connection deepened to the point where we initiated a podcast, "Heart2Heart2Moms: Finding Comfortable in the Uncomfortable," aiming to break the silence around child loss and offer a platform for shared healing. This project not only became a way to honor our daughters and share our journey with others but also served as a beacon of hope and understanding for those navigating the treacherous waters of grief. It underscored the importance of open dialogue about loss, a topic often shrouded in silence and highlighted the healing power of community.

Through our podcast, I learned the importance of expanding my support network to include not just those who have been there from the beginning but also those who, like Helen, brought fresh perspectives and unwavering understanding to my path of grief. Helen and I aim to break the silence surrounding child loss, offering comfort and connection to others. Our journey affirms the significance of building a 'Lemon Community'—a circle of support that embraces both the bitter and the sweet moments of life. This community is not just about shared grief but about the collective strength, healing, and the transformative power of opening up about our deepest pains and finding solace in shared experiences.

The story of how I navigated the aftermath of Madi's accident, the creation of our podcast, and the formation of the Lemon Community emphasizes the transformative power of connection. It highlights how reaching out, sharing our stories, and building networks of support can offer a pathway through grief, toward healing. This narrative is a testament to the strength found in vulnerability, the healing power of shared experiences, and the profound impact of creating spaces where the complexities of grief can be shared and understood.

Before we dive into these reflective questions, let us pause and squeeze every drop of insight from our experiences. I encourage you to open your *"Power of the Pause Journal"* and prepare to delve deep into your thoughts. This process, akin to transforming lemons into lemonade, allows you to use your journal as a tool to convert your reflections into clarity and insight. Through writing, we not only document our journey but also uncover new understandings and perspectives that might have remained unexplored. So, let us take this opportunity to reflect, write, and discover the profound lessons hidden within our life's challenges and triumphs.

Questions for Reflection

1. Who are the key members of your Lemon Community, and how have they supported you through different phases of your life?

2. Can you recall a time when sharing your experiences with others helped you see your situation in a new light? How did this impact your journey?

3. Think of a moment when being vulnerable with someone else led to a deeper connection or understanding. What did you learn from this experience?

4. How have you found comfort in uncomfortable or challenging situations? What role did others play in this process?

5. What steps can you take to expand your Lemon Community to include diverse perspectives and experiences? How might this benefit your personal growth and resilience?

As we conclude this chapter, I hope you find yourself more in tune with the resilience and beauty inherent in your Lemon Community. Remember this journey we are on, it is not meant to be walked alone. Our Lemon Community, a rich tapestry of longstanding friendships, newly forged bonds, and everything in between, adds depth and vibrancy to our existence. It offers us fortitude during the storms and amplifies our joy in the sunshine. So, continue to nurture those connections, share your story, and above all, fully engage with the myriad facets of this extraordinary journey called life. Together, within our Lemon Community, we will muster the strength to meet any challenge head-on, transforming obstacles into opportunities for growth and deeper connections.

CHAPTER 12

GRATEFUL REFLECTIONS

Cultivating a Resilient and Positive Spirit

In the journey that is life, taking moments to reflect on gratitude can be profoundly impactful. Gratitude is not reserved for the grandiose events that shake the very foundation of our existence. It is about tuning into a mindset that appreciates the good, both in monumental achievements and in the everyday experiences—the comforting aroma of coffee in the morning, an unexpected smile from a stranger, or a meaningful conversation with a friend. These instances of joy accumulate, crafting a life rich in appreciation and contentment.

During challenging times, such as when venturing into the realm of entrepreneurship or navigating the profound grief of losing Madison, focusing on things to be grateful for was a beacon in the night. It reminded me that, even on the hardest days, there are rays of positivity to hold onto. Whether it was the satisfaction from a successful business interaction, or the bittersweet comfort found in memories of Madison, gratitude grounded me, reminding me of the presence of love amidst loss and the opportunities for growth within challenges.

Cultivating an attitude of gratitude was not merely a temporary uplift but a practice that reinvigorated my spirit, provided clarity, and renewed my commitment to living each day with more intention. It propelled me through times of uncertainty, enriching my present and brightening my outlook on the future.

Resilience, much like a muscle, strengthens with use, becoming a critical ally in life's journey. It is what allows us to recover and say, *Let's do this*, despite the setbacks.

For me, resilience was built through action and clarity, especially during the transition from corporate life to entrepreneurship. It was about seizing my narrative, infusing my endeavors with passion, and finding fulfillment in the pursuit of new endeavors.

And amidst these experiences, it becomes essential to embrace our unique essence. Each of us has something extraordinary to offer—a combination of talents, quirks, and strengths that make us uniquely ourselves.

Embracing our story, living authentically, and approaching life with heart and intention is what makes us truly remarkable. It is not about striving for perfection but about being genuine, living with purpose, and allowing our true selves to shine through.

This chapter is a testament to the transformative power of gratitude and resilience, highlighting the importance of recognizing the beauty in life's simple pleasures and the strength in embracing our unique journeys. It is a reminder that, in the tapestry of life, every experience, whether joyous or challenging, contributes to the richness of our existence.

Cultivating Gratitude in Daily Life

❖ **Gratitude Reminders**: Set reminders to reflect on what you are thankful for, maybe at a certain time each day.

❖ **Mindful Moments**: Take time to appreciate your surroundings and current experiences, fully engaging in the present.

❖ **Notice the Little Things**: Pay attention to little joys daily – a kind gesture, a beautiful sunset, a favorite song.

❖ **Express Thankfulness**: Regularly express gratitude, whether through a journal, verbally, or by sending a thank you note.

❖ **Share the Positivity**: Spread gratitude by sharing what you are thankful for with others, enhancing not only your happiness but also theirs.

Cultivating a resilient, positive spirit requires nurturing much like caring for a garden. Begin by acknowledging the positive aspects that surround you daily. It is the small things that often bring the most joy, such as a serene morning, a satisfying meal, the laughter shared with a friend, or the comfort found in a favorite chair. These instances of gratitude act as beams of light, enriching your spirit and brightening your perspective on life.

Incorporate this practice into your daily routine. It could be writing down a few things you are grateful for in your journal, taking a moment of quiet reflection with your morning coffee, or sharing your grateful moments with family and friends to spread positivity. This habit not only bolsters your own sense of well-being but can also inspire those around you.

This approach is not about ignoring life's challenges but about finding a balance, recognizing the good amidst the struggles. By actively seeking out and appreciating the positive moments, you are training your mind to recognize and cherish these instances, fostering a spirit filled with resilience and joy that is firmly grounded in gratitude.

Paying attention to the positives around you can significantly shift your perspective, making you more aware of the joy and positivity that has always been present. It is like tuning the soundtrack of your life to play more feel-good tunes, allowing you to perceive opportunities where once there were only obstacles, and letting hope illuminate previously despair-filled spaces.

Embracing gratitude is more than a habit; it is a lifestyle choice that acknowledges and celebrates the goodness in our lives daily. It is about making a conscious decision to live fully, embracing each moment with enthusiasm and commitment to growth and happiness.

Moreover, the concept of "just being" emphasizes the importance of living in the present, not dwelling on the past or worrying about the future. This practice of mindfulness, especially significant during times of stress or grief, invites you to simply exist in the moment, embracing life as it unfolds. It is in these present moments that we find true connection with ourselves and the world around us, discovering the magic that life has to offer in the here and now.

Reflection

Consider incorporating more gratitude, resilience, and a positivity into your daily life. These small yet impactful steps can lead to significant transformations. So, take out your journal, and let us reflect on these questions to ignite change:

1. What are three aspects of your life you feel grateful for at this moment?
2. Look at a current challenge you are facing. Can you see it as an opportunity for growth? Describe how.
3. Recall a time when you showed resilience. What lessons did you learn from that experience?
4. What does 'being amazing' look like in your everyday life? What actions or attitudes embody this for you?
5. What is one positive change you can start implementing right now?

And here is the thing—life is more than just a series of days to get through; it is an opportunity for growth. By nurturing a heart full of gratitude, fostering a resilient spirit, and sprinkling your days with positivity, you can enhance this journey significantly. Let us use our moments of pause to uncover the silver linings in our experiences, crafting something beautiful from them. These reflections not only help us discover our true selves but also reveal our potential to thrive amidst life's twists and turns. Remember, life isn't just about living and surviving; it is about savoring each moment and loving the journey, with all its ups and downs.

PART 5

NURTURING THE PAUSE

MOVING AHEAD

CHAPTER 13

FROM LEMONS TO LESSONS

Moving Beyond the Pause

We do not always find ourselves in moments of pause, yet it is during these times we are given the chance to truly craft our path, to develop a plan that resonates deeply with our core. There is not a playbook or a set schedule for how we navigate these periods. Embracing creativity and stepping off the beaten track can sometimes feel overwhelming, especially when faced with the unknown.

Feeling stuck or unsure about taking the first step is a common experience when we are overwhelmed. This is when reaching out within your community, those folks who have been there, can help. They can offer support, or simply be there alongside you as you take that initial, daunting step. It is crucial to remember that we are all on our unique timelines, racing against no one but ourselves. Reminding ourselves that "Rome was not built in a day" can help keep us focused and moving forward at our own pace.

Life's journey is not about adhering strictly to a predetermined route; it is more about embracing the learning and growth that come with each step, and sometimes, taking a moment to step back and absorb the lessons life has to offer. Being gentle with ourselves, allowing for those necessary pauses, and staying true to who we are is vital. It is a daily effort to be authentic, especially in a world that is constantly watching.

Amanda Gorman's (2021) words, "There is always light if only we're brave enough to see it. If only we're brave enough to be it," serve as a powerful reminder that even in the darkest times, we can find or be the light for ourselves and others. It is about choosing to see the positives, no matter how small they may seem.

In moments of loss, the common advice is to "take as long as you need," yet it is peculiar how we seldom apply this understanding to other areas of our lives. Each pause, each quiet moment life offers us, comes with its own set of lessons. It is an opportunity to reflect, learn, and eventually, find our way forward with a renewed sense of purpose and resilience.

Reflecting on the significant moments of my journey reveals how each pause became a vital period of learning. Launching my business felt like I was jumping off a cliff and had to build my parachute on the way down. This journey taught me the importance of trusting my instincts and facing risks that felt right, even when they filled me with fear. There were days filled with doubt, but every hurdle taught me the value of persistence, encouraging me to push forward even when it seemed like everything was against me.

The loss of Madison, however, was an unparalleled experience. It plunged me into a depth of sorrow I had never experienced, revealing an inner strength I was unaware I possessed. This discovery was both surprising and empowering. Madison's memory became my beacon, teaching me to treasure each moment, to cling to the love we shared, and to seek meaning and purpose amidst the pain. This interruption in life was transformative, changing my view on life, love, and the fleeting nature of our time here.

Being true to oneself is crucial. Often, we find ourselves entangled in what others expect of us, yet the real essence of growth, especially during life's pauses, stems from authenticity. It is about following your heart and forging your path rather than conforming to the expectations laid out by others.

Life's pauses—whether they are the exhilarating challenges of starting a business or the profound sorrow of loss—have taught me the importance of introspection. It is about navigating through the noise of self-doubt and societal expectations to find what genuinely resonates with you. Authenticity is not merely about making choices that feel right; it is also about making choices that resonate with you, being kind to yourself, fully embracing every emotion, celebrating small victories, and learning from every experience.

These breaks in life, filled with tears, frustrations, and doubts, were not merely pauses; they were active periods of learning, reflection, and significant growth. They taught me about life's fragility, resilience's power, and the human spirit's strength. By understanding myself better, I have grown more empathetic, compassionate, and present, recognizing life's beauty every day. Embracing the lessons these pauses offer does not only help in moving forward; they profoundly enrich life. They enhance empathy, compassion, and a greater awareness of the present moment's beauty, reminding us of life's preciousness.

So, when life hits the pause button for you, seek out those hidden lessons. They are there, in every challenge, waiting to reveal themselves and help you grow. Remember, it is precisely these pauses, as daunting and complex as they might be, that mold us into who we are meant to be.

Lessons in Kindness and Letting Go

Being kind to oneself is a vital lesson. It is all too common to be one's own harshest critic, pushing oneself to the limit and reproaching oneself for not achieving more. However, learning the power of kindness—the gentle, compassionate internal voice that reassures you that it is okay to take the time you need, that you are actually performing better than you think—is the real key to progress. It is about extending the same grace and understanding to oneself that you would offer to a close friend. This kindness allows us to navigate challenging times with a measure of gentleness and a great deal of fortitude.

Let us also consider the pauses and challenges that are part of life. They are not mere obstacles; they are replete with valuable lessons that may not be immediately evident. Each challenge and pause in life brings a spark of insight and the opportunity for growth. Finding the value in a challenge is akin to searching for a ray of sunshine on an overcast day—it might require a closer look, but it is always there. Every challenge also teaches a lesson in disguise, whether it is about patience, building resilience, or learning the art of letting go.

Letting go is admittedly a struggle I face every single day. It can be about releasing old ways that do not benefit me anymore, or confronting fears of what is to come. It is a continuous process, a path of personal evolution. Every day serves as a reminder that letting go is crucial for moving ahead, for personal growth and transformation. It is about shifting focus from what I cannot influence to what is within my power to change. This struggle, while constant, has taught me that there is liberty and opportunity in releasing what I cannot control. As I persist on this journey, I hold this lesson dear, knowing that every effort to let go is a stride toward a more authentic, free self. This practice of release is integral to embracing life wholeheartedly and passionately.

Embracing a positive outlook in the midst of hardship is not about denial of pain or struggle. It is about embracing the entirety of our experiences and growing from them. It is understanding that each challenge presents a chance for advancement, an opening to become more resilient, wiser, and more attuned to oneself and one's life journey.

So, when faced with life's inevitable pauses or obstacles, the key is kindness to oneself. Seek out the lessons that are waiting to be discovered. They are present, often hidden within the challenges themselves, ready to guide us toward personal growth and transformation.

During those deeply challenging times when it felt like everything was caving in, I discovered unexpected sources of light that I had not noticed before. My community, my group of steadfast supporters, shone brightly, providing comfort and strength. Every kind word, every cherished memory shared, and just uttering Madison's name brought immense solace. Their unwavering presence was a constant reminder that I was not navigating through the darkness alone.

The memories of Madison are treasured jewels, each one shining with the love and joy we shared, offering solace when grief becomes too heavy. These recollections are a sanctuary, affirming the enduring nature of love. It persists, accompanies, and illuminates the path forward.

The progress in my business, no matter how minor it seemed, contributed significantly to overcoming challenges. Each accomplishment, each advance, sparked light amidst the shadows. To the outside world, these might have seemed minor, but for me, they were monumental affirmations that even amidst sorrow and uncertainty, there was still room for growth and progress.

These beacons of light guided me through tumultuous times, leading to a place where the seeds of hope could germinate once again. It was a period of rediscovery, relearning how to find light even in the darkest moments. This journey taught me that even when life seems overwhelmingly dark, there are always spots of light if we look for them. These glimmers of hope can guide us onto new paths of hope, healing, and fresh starts.

Transforming Challenges into Opportunities for Growth

Reflecting on life's pauses and the lessons they have imparted is a deeply personal exercise.

Consider the following:

❖ Think about the significant pauses you faced and the insights you gained.

❖ Reflect on how these pauses have contributed to your growth and how you have evolved beyond them.

❖ Think about how you can apply the wisdom from these experiences to your future path.

Grab your journal and write down your thoughts. Reflect on your lessons learned, the growth you experienced, and how you moved beyond each pause. Then think about how you can apply these lessons to your journey ahead.

1. What was a "lemon" moment in your life and what valuable lesson did it teach you?

2. In what ways do you stay true to yourself and show kindness in your day-to-day life?

3. Can you recall a time when a challenge revealed an unexpected positive outcome or insight? How did that feel?

4. Describe how you envision moving forward from a current or past pause in your life. What does that journey look like and feel like?

5. How can you use the insights gained from your life's pauses to navigate future challenges or seize new opportunities?

Life's pauses, those moments where everything seems to stand still, they are not just gaps in our journey—they are fertile grounds for growth, self-discovery, and transformation. Every pause offers an opportunity to reflect, to reassess, and to emerge more authentically ourselves. Embrace these moments, cherish them, and let the lessons they teach propel you forward.

With each challenge, with each pause life presents, there is a chance to become stronger, more enlightened, and resilient. So, as you face the lemons life throws your way, remember that within them lie the seeds of wisdom, of lessons waiting to be discovered and cherished. Let us absorb every lesson, relish every moment, and make the most of every pause we encounter.

This journey, with all its twists and turns, its pauses and plays, is ours to embrace—let us do so wholeheartedly, transforming every lemon into a lesson that enriches our path forward.

CHAPTER 14

MADISON'S LEGACY

The Metamorphosis of Hope

In this remarkable journey we call life, the most profound lessons are often whispered to us by nature's most delicate and graceful beings. We can take a moment to consider the butterfly. This creature is not merely an insect fluttering by; it embodies transformation, a testament to nature's miraculous ability to change. Picture it—a humble caterpillar, once bound to the earth, confined to its immediate surroundings, undergoes an incredible metamorphosis. It emerges as a breathtaking butterfly, free to dance in the air and explore the world from an entirely new perspective.

This transformation mirrors the power of the pause in our lives. It is a profound evolution. Just as the caterpillar encases itself in a cocoon, we too often find ourselves wrapped in life's pauses, cocooned in moments of self-reflection, challenge, and change. It is in these moments that we are given the opportunity to grow, to develop our wings in the quiet, unseen moments.

The process is not always easy. Just like the caterpillar's metamorphosis, our transformations can be filled with struggle and discomfort. But it is through this process that we gain our wings, our ability to rise above and see life from a new vantage point. It is a journey of not just physical, but also emotional and spiritual unfolding, where we stretch our capabilities and discover our true potential.

In the quiet of our cocoon—our pause—we may feel isolated, uncertain of what is to come. Yet, it is here, in this space, where we do the most significant work of our lives. We weave the fabric of our future selves, thread by thread, day by day, until we are ready to break free and reveal our new form to the world.

The butterfly's journey from crawling to soaring is a powerful reminder that every phase of our life, every pause, holds the potential for incredible transformation. It is a message of hope and resilience, urging us to embrace our periods of growth, however challenging they may be. For it is through these periods that we learn not just to walk, not just to crawl, but to spread our wings and fly.

A few months after Madison's passing, I experienced a profound moment with a butterfly. Upstairs in Madison's room, I was overwhelmed with grief, expressing my longing to hold her once more. As I descended the stairs, a butterfly caught my attention outside our window, resting on a plant. My heart leaped at the sight. Rushing outside, I came face-to-face with this mesmerizing creature.

For the first time, I touched a butterfly. As I caressed her wings, I felt enveloped in Madison's warmth, whispering to her presence felt in the flutter. Those moments, sharing a connection with the butterfly, felt like a direct bond with Madison, a magical and unforgettable experience that I hold dear.

Every encounter with a butterfly, allowing me the honor of closeness, feels like a tender message from Madison. In their silent flight, I sense a connection, as if Madison reassures and guides me, urging me to appreciate life's beauty and fragility. These moments are not mere coincidences but are poignant reminders of our everlasting bond, transcending the physical world.

The way these butterflies appear, often precisely when I need them most, feels like a miracle. Whether I am lost in thought, wrestling with grief, or just moving through my day, their arrival brings a comforting presence, piercing through the darkness. It is as if Madison responds directly to me, answering my silent calls and questions. These moments offer a pause, an opportunity to breathe deeply, to smile, and to immerse myself in the warmth of Madison's endless love.

It is incredible, isn't it? How nature can be our greatest teacher, how a tiny butterfly can embody such immense lessons about love, loss, and the enduring connections. They teach me about resilience, the strength to keep going, and the courage to take on each new day with hope and grace.

In these fluttering creatures, I find a powerful metaphor for my own journey. Like them, I am learning to navigate through my own transformations, embracing periods of growth and change. They inspire me to spread my wings, explore new horizons, and to find joy in the journey, no matter how challenging it may be.

Madison's butterflies have become symbols of my journey forward, a journey of healing, discovery, and continuous growth. With each sighting, with each gentle flutter, I am reminded of the endless cycle of life, of renewal, and of the incredible strength and beauty that lies within us all. So, as I continue on this path, I carry these encounters close to my heart, letting them guide me, inspire me, and remind me that in every moment of pause, there is an opportunity to flutter forward, just like Madison's beautiful butterflies.

And then, there it is, that pivotal moment, just like the butterfly, when it is time to step out and show the world the incredible transformation we have gone through. It is way more than just the outward change, it is the dazzle of new colors, it it's the story behind them, the resilience it took to build them, the personal growth that happened in those quiet, unseen moments.

Consider this—when we finally spread our wings, it is our silent way of sharing our journey. It is our message to the world: "This is my story; this is who I've become." It is about embracing every challenge that has shaped us and coming out on the other side in readiness to soar, and to truly live life.

Spreading our wings is an act of declaration. It declares our triumph over trials, our evolution into something magnificent. It is not just showing a new exterior; it is showcasing our resilience, our bravery, the perseverance that carried us through the difficult times.

As we embark on our first flight with these new wings, let us honor the journey that led us here. Every tough decision, every tear shed, every moment of uncertainty, contributed to the strength of our wings. We soar not in spite of our past, but because of it. This flight represents a blend of our experiences—our past, our present, and our future.

When it is your time to emerge and unfold your wings, seize it wholeheartedly. Celebrate the transformations you have navigated, the resilience you have forged, and the growth you have attained. It is your moment to dazzle, to explore, to revel in life from a fresh, thrilling perspective. Like the butterfly, make every second count, transform each pause into a bold leap towards the heavens. Your wings are a testament to your journey, with every hue narrating the uniqueness of your path.

Madison's butterflies serve as a reminder of life's cycles—of change, rejuvenation, and new beginnings. They signify that even in the darkest moments, there is potential for light, beauty, and fresh starts. They show that growth often sprouts from unexpected places, and sometimes, a pause is all it takes to ready ourselves for the next chapter of our lives.

When you find yourself in a moment of transformation, view it as your opportunity to evolve, change, and prepare for what is next. Cherish this phase, and when you are ready, embrace your journey with the grace and resilience of a butterfly taking flight. Like the butterflies that Madison cherished, you possess the strength and beauty to rise above and move forward.

Now, take a moment to reach for your journal. This is your sanctuary for reflection, a place to pen down your growth, transformations, and the pivotal moments of change in your life. Let your journal be a haven where your thoughts and experiences can unfold and soar, much like the symbolic butterflies that represent change and new beginnings. Ask yourself the following questions:

1. Reflect on a moment in your life that marked a profound personal change. How did this period transform you?

2. Have you ever experienced a natural symbol, such as a butterfly, which signified change or transformation in your life? Describe this symbol and its impact.

3. Identify your "butterfly garden" - a specific place or activity that provides you with peace and tranquility. What makes this place or activity special to you?

4. Share an important lesson about change that you have learned from the natural world. How has this lesson influenced your perspective or actions?

5. In what ways do you acknowledge and celebrate your personal growth in day-to-day life?

As I conclude this section, I share a glimpse into a special place of mine—my butterfly garden. This tranquil spot in my backyard serves as a living showcase of life's cycles, from the humble beginnings of caterpillars to the emergence of vibrant butterflies. It is a vivid reminder of nature's marvels and feels like a gentle nod from Madison. Amid the greenery, a sign stands, reading, "Butterflies from Madison," bringing a personal touch that brightens my day every time I catch sight of it.

The transformation of caterpillars into magnificent butterflies within this garden fills me with a profound sense of joy. It symbolizes renewal, the beauty inherent in change, and the enduring bond I have with Madison. Each butterfly that takes flight, every blossom that unfurls, seems to carry her spirit, infusing the space with love and joy.

This garden is more than a place of natural beauty; it is where I feel a deep connection to Madison, a sanctuary for reflection on the path we have journeyed, and the insights gained. It offers comfort, peace, and a constant reminder of life's wonders.

As you navigate your own path, I encourage you to find your "butterfly garden"—be it a literal place or an activity that brings you happiness and serenity. Welcome the changes in your life, appreciate the growth, and remain open to the delightful surprises nature offers. Let your experiences enrich you with joy and see the world with the wonder and freedom of a butterfly in the wind. Here is to moving forward, with hearts light and spirits soaring.

EPILOGUE

JOURNEYING TOGETHER

From Life's Pauses to Purposeful Paths

Friends, we have reached a heartfelt milestone in our journey together. It is time to take a deep breath, pause, and soak in the gratitude. I am truly thankful for your companionship on this adventure. Choosing my book, walking this path alongside me, and weaving your stories with mine has been a blessing. Your support has shone brightly, bringing comfort and happiness along the way. You have been an essential part of this life chapter, and for that, I offer my deepest thanks.

Your journey alongside me has been filled with every shade of emotion, from laughter to tears and everything in between. I am so grateful for your presence on this incredible ride. Together, we shared more than just stories; we truly lived life side by side, learning and growing every step of the way.

Reflecting on the path we traveled, from the intense days in the finance world to the heart-wrenching transition of my dear Madison, it has been an odyssey of significant moments. Each major decision, whether it was changing careers or embracing a new beginning, has been a landmark in my journey of self-discovery. These are not just events; they have been transformative, shaping my understanding of my true self.

Therefore, as we move forward into the next stage of our lives, let us envision it as a butterfly's transformation—beautiful and continuously evolving. My encouragement to you is to take the unexpected challenges life throws your way and use them as a catalyst for a journey of courage, change, and limitless possibilities.

TURNING GRIEF INTO ACTION

The Birth of Madi's Movement -

A Path Forward for Foster Teens

The loss of Madison was not just a brief stop in life's journey; it became a profound event that reshaped my whole being. In the silence that ensued, I discovered a reservoir of strength previously untapped. This newfound strength became the foundation of "Madi's Movement," a mission dedicated to fulfilling Madi's vision of empowering foster teens, especially those on the brink of adulthood without a safety net. This initiative is not merely a side project; it has woven itself into the fabric of my identity, turning profound grief into a legacy brimming with hope and a commitment to improve the lives of others.

The Turning Point: From TEDx to Present Day

It is almost beyond belief, right? As we approached a year without Madison, I found myself on a TEDx stage, sharing my story with an openness that was both terrifying and therapeutic. That day marked a turning point, stirring something deep within me. This very book is born from that pivotal moment, nurtured into being by the support of those who listened, my cherished family and friends, and

Lester's steadfast belief in me. It stands as a testament to my quest to touch lives and enact positive change in the world.

Heart2Heart2Moms: Sharing and Healing

I teamed up with Helen to create something truly special, "Heart2Heart2Moms: Finding Comfort in the Uncomfortable." It is our podcast, a place for those deep, meaningful conversations. We delve into the challenging topics of loss and resilience, alongside the powerful connections that keep us upright amidst life's tumult. This podcast is our way of healing together, offering a mutual understanding, and that comforting reassurance that we are not alone in this journey. It is about providing a space where healing is shared, understanding is mutual, and everyone feels that, despite the discomfort, there is a community of support.

Building Our Lemon Community

Think of your Lemon Community as your personal cheer squad. These people are the pillars in your life, always there to lend an ear or a helping hand through every twist and turn. They are the ones who celebrate your wins, big or small, and stand with you when you face those tough moments, whether you are turning sour moments into something sweet, or just need a friend to lean on, they are here for you, every step of the way.

Explore **www.EffieSantos.com** and connect with us across all social media platforms **@Effie Santos.** Dive into a community that is buzzing with support, inspiration, and resources you need to thrive.

With the Lemon Community by your side, you are never alone; let us be your guide and support.

Join us and share your story, your journey—with its pauses and successes—and discover how together, we can make every part of life a little bit sweeter. Let's share our stories and experiences, celebrate every victory, and support each other along the way. Together, we are unstoppable! We look forward to welcoming you!

Effie Santos: A NEW CHAPTER BEGINS

Now, let us unveil something truly close to my heart – my journey as Effie Santos, fully embracing this new chapter that life has handed me. This pause, this moment of quiet and introspection, has been nothing short of a reset, a chance to dive deep and emerge truly aligned with my purpose. It is like I found my spot, exactly where I need to be. With this new beginning, I am dedicating myself to sharing my story, my lessons, and my heart across stages, podcasts, and any platform where my voice can reach those in need. My goal is to foster a community of connection, growth, and mutual support. This path I am on is all about impact – lending a hand to those grappling with grief, facing life's complex challenges, or anyone just looking for a beacon to help find their way. That is my mission, and you know what? We are already on our way.

The Next Chapter: Stay Tuned For My Next Book

Stay tuned for my next book - *She Didn't Make It: Grieving, Growing, and Grasping Beyond* - where I will share more about my spiritual journey and the signs from Madison, showing that our connection is as strong as ever. As I continue to navigate this journey of healing and growth, each page will unveil new insights, moments of clarity, and profound encounters that illuminate the path forward. The story is still unfolding, with each chapter revealing the depth of our connection and the enduring impact of our shared experiences. I cannot wait to share it with you.

I invite you to stay connected and follow along on our journey. Visit my website www.effiesantos.com, follow our social media updates, and engage with everything Effie Santos, Madi's Movement, and Heart2Heart2Moms have to offer.

Keep in touch, because there is much more on the horizon that I am eager to explore together.

ACKNOWLEDGEMENTS

Reflecting on the journey of creating this book brings to light the incredible circle of souls who have been instrumental in its realization. Ellen Patterson, beyond being an editor, you have been a beacon of friendship, guiding me with wisdom and standing by me with unwavering support. You have become an integral part of our family circle.

From childhood to now, watching you grow up alongside Athena and Madi has made you more than Athena's best friend; you are a daughter to me, Geni. Thank you for being an inseparable part of our family, sharing in every joy and every challenge, and for all the support and cherished moments. You mean the world to us.

Gwen, as my publisher and editor, your nurturing guidance and empathetic understanding have been my anchor through the tumultuous phases of this journey. Your patience and kindness have illuminated the path forward, making a significant difference in both the book and my personal growth.

To my dear friends who have been my pillars in the darkest times, your support has been nothing short of a blessing. You have carried my burdens alongside me, lent an ear to my fears, and rejoiced in my triumphs. I am eternally grateful for the depth and strength of our friendship.

I extend my heartfelt embrace to everyone who has touched my life and this book in myriad ways— to all the readers and audiences who have resonated with my message. Your engagement and feedback have been invaluable, enriching this journey beyond words.

This book mirrors not only my personal experiences but also the collective love, support, and connectivity we share as a community. My deepest gratitude goes out to each of you for being an essential part of this incredible journey. Here is to the new horizons that await us, and to the brilliant moments yet to be discovered in our stories. Let us harness our challenges not only to create sweetness but also to plant seeds for new beginnings, revelations, and transformative changes.

With all my love and anticipation for the adventures that lie ahead,

ES

REFERENCES

Gorman, Amanda (January 22, 2021) - Poet Amanda Gorman Speaks at the Biden-Harris Inauguration 2021: *The Hill We Climb.* From: https://youtu.be/_U6IKviDWFs

Miller, Joel and Alan (2021) – p. 46. The Sky Floor: *You Don't Have to be Amazing to Start.* From: https://www.theskyfloor.com/you-dont-have-to-be-amazing-to-start/

Forbes (June 5, 2018) – Leadership: *5 Things You Need To Know About Women In Finance.* From:
https://www.forbes.com/sites/forbesmarketplace/2018/06/05
5-things-you-need-to-know-about-women-in
finance/?sh=c201bf44e776

Johnen, Becky (May 13, 2018) – Facing the Sunshine and Avoiding the Shadows: *Elbert Hubbard.* From:
https://authorbeckyjohnen.wordpress.com/tag/elbert-hubbard/

O.T. Genasis - (2021) - I Look Good Today : *I Look Real Good Today. From: https://www.youtube.com/watch?v=KU-RQeAC9os*

www.ingramcontent.com/pod-product-compliance
Lightning Source LLC
Chambersburg PA
CBHW070636030426

42337CB00020B/4032